The Complete

F.A. Amateur Cup

Results Book

AUTHOR
Richard Samuel

Price
£8.95

British Library Cataloguing in Publication Data
A catalogue record for this book is available from the British Library
ISBN 1-86223-066-8

Copyright © 2003   SOCCER BOOKS LIMITED (01472-696226)
72, St. Peters' Avenue, Cleethorpes, N.E. Lincolnshire, DN35 8HU, England

Printed by 4edge Ltd. www.4edge.co.uk

A Brief History of the F.A. Amateur Cup

The founding of the English Football League in 1888 created a tremendous upsurge in the popularity of the sport at all levels. The following year, clubs which had unsuccessfully applied for membership of the Football League formed the Football Alliance which, itself, was integrated into the Football League as the Second Division in 1892 and the 'professional' game, as we know it, was born.

This professionalism soon resulted in a decline in the performances of amateur clubs in the much-loved F.A. Cup competition and, in August 1892, the country's oldest club, Sheffield FC, offered to provide a cup for which amateur clubs alone could compete. Although this generous offer was declined by the Football Association, in February 1893 they resolved to commence the competition in the October of that year. The competition rules which were drawn up were almost the same as those for the F.A. Cup itself.

Thus was the F.A. Amateur Cup born and, in August 1893, the Football Association set up it's Amateur Cup Sub-Committee under the chairmanship of N.L. Jackson who set about purchasing a suitable trophy. By today's standards the amount paid for the magnificent trophy (£30.00) seems a trifling sum but it should be remembered that, at that time, a farm labourer's annual wage was only £25.00!

Eighty-one clubs competed in the inaugural competition and, to reduce the number to a manageable 32 clubs, a qualifying competition kicked-off on 21st October 1893 when 16 clubs met in the first qualifying round. In fact, 18 clubs were due to play that day but Clapton withdrew, presumably being unable to afford the costs of travelling to play their opponents in Norwich. Indeed, this set the pattern for many early ties when a club would often scratch to avoid incurring heavy travelling fares. This seems a little strange today but was perfectly in keeping with the F.A. Cup itself where such clubs as Glasgow Celtic pulled out of ties to avoid the costs too!

In the second year of the competition, it was decided that the 32 clubs to compete would consist of the four semi-finalists from the previous year's competition plus 20 other leading clubs with the remaining eight places falling to the winners of the eight regional divisions. This pattern continued throughout the time of the competition although the numbers of qualifying divisions increased as the numbers of entrants increased.

The early years of the competition were much dominated by the 'old boys' teams from public schools but, when the Arthur Dunn Cup kicked-off in 1902-03, they forsook the F.A. Amateur Cup and competed there instead.

Between the wars southern clubs dominated the competition and attendances at Cup Finals rose to extraordinary numbers (35,000 in 1928-29) but it was only after the Second World War that the real upsurge took place with the move to Wembley in 1949. Thereafter, the golden years of the competition saw sell-out Wembley Finals with crowds of 100,000 for a number of years before a slow decline started in the late 1950's.

When the Football Association decided to dispense with the term 'Amateur' in 1974, Final attendances had dropped to around 30,000 and the time had come to draw a curtain on a magnificent tournament which had ranked second only to the F.A. Cup in prestige and following.

N.L. Jackson, Esq.

A former Vice-President of the Football Association who oversaw the creation of the competition as the chairman of the F.A. Amateur Cup Sub-Committee.

1893-94 Amateur Cup

First Qualifying Round

Dover vs Sheppey United	1-4
Erith vs Cray Wanderers	0-3
Maidenhead vs Old Weymouthians	2-1
New Brompton vs Maidstone	7-0
Norwich Thorpe walk-over (Clapton scratched)	
Old Foresters vs Swifts	2-1
Reading vs Chesham	4-0
Sittingbourne vs Royal Engineers	1-2
Windsor & Eton vs Freemantle	0-5

Second Qualifying Round

Ashford vs Folkestone	0-6
Beeston vs Lincoln Lindum	8-0
Berwick Rangers walk-over (St. Hilda's scratched)	
Bristol St. George vs Warmley	1-0
Clapham Rovers vs Crouch End	2-0
Cray Wanderers vs Royal Ordnance Factories	0-3
Darlington St. Augustine's vs Willington Athletic	2-3
Home Park (Plymouth) walk-over (Bedminster scratched)	
Ilford vs Ipswich Town	1-0
Kendal vs Ashington	2-4
Leadgate Ark vs Leadgate Exiles	0-1
Loftus vs Scarborough	4-2
Maidenhead vs Freemantle	3-1
New Brompton vs Royal Fusiliers	2-0
Norwich Thorpe vs West Herts	2-6
Old Foresters vs Old St. Stephen's	0-1
Old St. Mark's vs Old Harrovians	3-2
Old Wykehamists vs Cranleighians	6-1
Reading vs Chesham Generals	2-1
Royal Engineers vs Sheppey United	1-4
Rushden vs Hunts County	12-1
Saltburn Swifts vs South Bank	4-6
South Bank Blue Star vs North Skelton Rovers	4-0
Surbiton Hill vs Old Etonians	0-5
Tottenham Hotspur vs Vampires	3-1
Whitby walk-over (Scarborough Rangers scratched)	
Wellingborough Town	bye

Third Qualifying Round

Beeston	bye
Berwick Rangers vs Leadgate Exiles	1-2
Clapham Rovers walk-over (Tottenham Hotspur were suspended)	
Folkestone vs Sheppey United	1-1
Home Park (Plymouth) vs Bristol St. George	2-1
Ilford vs West Herts	2-0
New Brompton vs Royal Ordnance Factories	1-2
Old St. Mark's vs Old Etonians	2-5
Old Wykehamists vs Old St. Stephen's	3-4
Reading vs Maidenhead	3-3

South Bank vs South Bank Blue Star	2-0
Wellingborough Town vs Rushden	1-4
Whitby vs Loftus	2-0
Willington Athletic vs Ashington	4-0
Rhos received a bye	
Warrington St. Elphin's received a bye	

Third Qualifying Round Replays

Maidenhead vs Reading	0-4
Sheppey United vs Folkestone	2-1

Third Qualifying Round 2nd Replay

Maidenhead vs Reading (after a protest) (at Maidenhead)	3-4

First Round

Bishop Auckland walk-over (Clapham Rovers scratched)	
Casuals vs Sheffield	3-1
Chatham vs Willington Athletic	1-0
Chirk vs South Bank	3-1
Great Marlow vs Darlington	1-0
Ilford vs Whitby	2-1
Middlesbrough vs Leadgate Exiles	8-0
Old Brightonians walk-over (Old Westminsters scratched)	
Old Carthusians vs Crusaders	4-2
Old St. Stephen's walk-over (Warrington St. Elphin's scratched)	
Reading vs Royal Ordnance Factories	3-2
Rhos vs Rushden	2-4
Sheppey United vs Old Etonians	1-3
Sherwood Foresters vs Colchester	2-1
Shrewsbury Town vs Beeston	5-2
Stockton vs Home Park (Plymouth)	5-0

Second Round

Bishop Auckland vs Ilford	4-2
Chatham vs Casuals	0-2
Chirk vs Old Brightonians	4-3
Great Marlow vs Rushden	2-0
Old Etonians vs Middlesbrough	4-2
Old St. Stephen's vs Shrewsbury Town	2-2
Reading vs Old Carthusians	1-4
Sherwood Foresters vs Stockton	1-4

Second Round Replay

Shrewsbury Town vs Old St. Stephen's	4-0

Third Round

Bishop Auckland vs Shrewsbury Town	3-1
Casuals walk-over (Chirk scratched)	
Old Etonians vs Sherwood Foresters	2-5
Old Carthusians vs Great Marlow	4-1

Semi-Finals

Sherwood Foresters vs Casuals	0-1
(at Leyton)	
Old Carthusians vs Bishop Auckland	5-1
(at Nottingham)	

Final

Old Carthusians vs Casuals	2-1
(at Athletic Ground, Richmond 7 April 1894)	

Attendance: 3,500

Old Carthusians: Wilkinson, Walters, Bray, Bliss, Wreford Brown, Streatfield, Hewitt, Richardson, Buzzard, Wilson, Stanborough
Scorers: Buzzard, Stanborough
Casuals: Harrison, Lodge, Hatton, Barker, A. Topham, Grierson, R. Topham, Carlton, Perkins, T. Rhodes, W. Rhodes
Scorer: R. Topham
Referee: T. Gunning (London)

1894-95 Amateur Cup

First Round

Beeston vs Tottenham Hotspur	0-2
Bishop Auckland vs Middlesbrough	2-3
Clapton vs King's Own Lancashire Regiment	0-4
Cliftonville vs Buxton	2-0
Crewe Alexandra vs Sheffield	7-0
Crusaders walk-over (Chatham scratched)	
Darlington vs Saltburn Swifts	3-2
Ealing vs Great Marlow	3-4
Ipswich Town vs 2nd Battalion Scots Guards	0-0
Leek vs Shrewsbury Town	3-3
Maidenhead vs Old Brightonians	2-4
Old Carthusians walk-over (Swindon scratched)	
Old Etonians walk-over (Sittingbourne scratched)	
Old Westminsters walk-over (Sheppey scratched)	
Reading vs Casuals	3-1
Stockton vs South Bank	3-0*, 1-3
* match abandoned	

First Round Replays

Ipswich Town vs 2nd Battalion Scots Guards	2-1
Shrewsbury Town vs Leek	2-0

Second Round

Crewe Alexandra vs Shrewsbury Town	2-0
Darlington vs Middlesbrough	1-1
Great Marlow vs King's Own Lancashire Regiment	2-4
Ipswich Town vs Old Etonians	1-1
Old Brightonians walk-over (Crusaders scratched)	
Reading vs Old Westminsters	8-2

South Bank walk-over (Cliftonville scratched)	
Tottenham Hotspur vs Old Carthusians	0-5

Second Round Replays

Middlesbrough vs Darlington	1-1
Old Etonians vs Ipswich Town	7-3

Second Round Second Replay

Middlesbrough vs Darlington	2-0
(at Middlesbrough)	

Third Round

King's Own Lancashire Regiment walk-over (Old Etonians scratched)	
Old Brightonians vs Middlesbrough	0-8
Old Carthusians vs Crewe Alexandra	1-0
South Bank vs Reading	5-2

Semi-Finals

Middlesbrough vs King's Own Lancashire Regiment	4-0
(at Derby)	
South Bank vs Old Carthusians	1-1
(at Leeds)	

Semi-Final Replay

South Bank vs Old Carthusians	2-3
(at Derby)	

Final

Middlesbrough vs Old Carthusians	2-1
(at Headingley, Leeds 27 April 1895)	

Attendance: 4,000

Middlesbrough: Cooper, Piercy, D. Wilson, Allport, Morren, Bache, Johnson, Gittens, Mullen, Nelmes, Murphy
Scorers: Mullen, Nelmes
Old Carthusians: Wilkinson, A. Walters, P. Walters, Buzzard, Kite, Streatfield, Hewitt, Broadbent, Smith, C. Wilson, Stanborough
Scorer: Smith
Referee: R. Lythgoe (Liverpool)

1895-96 Amateur Cup

First Round

Barking Woodville vs Royal Scot Fusiliers	1-3
Casuals vs Shrewsbury Town	2-4
Chesham Generals walk-over (Tottenham Hotspur disqualified)	
Darlington vs Whitby	2-0
Eastbourne vs Old Brightonians	2-5

Great Marlow vs Wycombe Wanderers	3-2
Hunslet vs Buxton	3-1
Ipswich Town vs Old Harrovians	6-2
Maidenhead vs London Welsh	0-1*, 3-4†
* match abandoned † London Welsh disqualified	
Middlesbrough vs Willington Athletic	6-2
Royal Artillery (Portsmouth) versus	
3rd Battalion Grenadier Guards	1-1
Sheffield vs Bishop Auckland	3-4
Old Carthusians walk-over (Oxford City scratched)	
Old Etonians walk-over (Leek scratched)	
Stockton vs South Bank	4-3
West Herts vs Wolverton L.N.W.R. Works	4-3

First Round Replay

3rd Battalion Grenadier Guards versus	
Royal Artillery (Portsmouth)	2-2

First Round Second Replay

Royal Artillery (Portsmouth) versus	
3rd Battalion Grenadier Guards	1-0
(at Guildford)	

Second Round

Bishop Auckland vs Ipswich Town	3-1
Great Marlow vs Chesham Generals	1-0
Hunslet vs Old Etonians	3-2
Maidenhead vs West Herts	1-0
Middlesbrough vs Royal Artillery (Portsmouth)	1-2
Old Carthusians vs Darlington	1-1
Royal Scots Fusiliers vs Stockton	1-4
Shrewsbury Town vs Old Brightonians	6-2

Second Round Replay

Darlington vs Old Carthusians	4-3

Third Round

Bishop Auckland vs Stockton	2-1
Darlington vs Hunslet	6-0
Great Marlow vs Shrewsbury	1-2
Maidenhead vs Royal Artillery (Portsmouth)	0-5

Semi-Finals

Bishop Auckland vs Darlington	3-2
(at Middlesbrough)	
Royal Artillery (Portsmouth) vs Shrewsbury Town	2-0
(at Reading)	

Final

Bishop Auckland vs Royal Artillery (Portsmouth)	1-0
(at Walnut Street, Leicester 28 March 1896)	

Attendance: 3,000

Bishop Auckland: Ward, Pennington, Tuson, Marshall, Lunson, Adams, Lewin, Lodge, Foster, Wilson, Manners
Scorer: Lodge
Royal Artillery (Portsmouth): Reilly, Phillips, Harris, Patterson, Hill, Kininan, Jardine, Hanna, Cook, Walsh, Meggs
Referee: A. Roston Bourke (London)

1896-97 Amateur Cup

First Round

Bishop Auckland vs Town Law	1-0
Bristol South End vs Old Carthusians	0-10
Cheshunt vs Old Brightonians	1-3
Darlington vs Thornaby Utopians	3-2
2nd East Lancashire Regiment (Aldershot) versus	
3rd Grenadier Guards	3-1
Ipswich Town vs Ealing	1-3
Kirkley vs Old Weymouthians	5-1
Leadgate Park vs Whitby	1-0
Leytonstone vs Faversham	4-3
Old Etonians vs Royal Artillery (Portsmouth)	2-3
Old Wilsonians vs Hunslet	0-6
Maidenhead vs Old Westminsters	0-2
Shankhouse vs Middlesbrough	3-1
Stockton vs South Bank	4-0†, 2-0
† after a protest	
Wandsworth vs Great Marlow	1-6
Wycombe Wanderers vs Casuals	3-5

Second Round

Bishop Auckland vs Hunslet	4-0
Casuals vs Royal Artillery (Portsmouth)	3-2
Darlington vs Stockton	4-6
Leadgate Park vs Shankhouse	3-1
Leytonstone vs Great Marlow	2-6
Old Brightonians vs Kirkley	0-2
Old Carthusians vs Ealing	2-1
Old Westminsters versus	
2nd East Lancashire Regiment (Aldershot)	4-1

Third Round

Great Marlow vs Kirkley	1-1
Leadgate Park vs Bishop Auckland	2-0
Old Carthusians vs Old Westminsters	3-1
Stockton vs Casuals	4-0

Third Round Replay

Kirkley vs Great Marlow	1-0*
* Kirkley were disqualified	

Semi-Finals

Great Marlow vs Old Carthusians (at Leyton)	0-0
Stockton vs Leadgate Park (at Middlesbrough)	2-0

Semi-Final Replay

Great Marlow vs Old Carthusians (at Maidenhead)	1-2

Final

Old Carthusians vs Stockton (at Tufnell Park, London 27 March 1897)	1-1

Attendance: 9,000

Old Carthusians: Wilkinson, Bray, Timmins, Bliss, Wreford Brown, Darvell, G. Wilson, Buzzard, Smith, Stanborough, Hewitt
Scorer: Smith
Stockton: Hamilton, Brannen, C. Wilson, Shaw, Murray, Monteith, Robson, Daniel, Addison, Sanderson, Lakey
Scorer: Sanderson
Referee: A. Kingscott (Derby)

Final Replay

Stockton vs Old Carthusians (at Feethams Ground, Darlington 17 April 1897)	1-4

Attendance: 10,000

Old Carthusians: Wilkinson, Bray, Timmins, Darvell, Wreford-Brown, Bliss, Hewitt, Buzzard, Smith, Stanborough, Jameson
Scorers: Hewitt, Stanborough, Buzzard, Smith
Stockton: Hamilton, Brannen, C. Wilson, Shaw, Murray, Monteith, Robson, Lee, Halfpenny, Sanderson, Lakey
Scorer: Halfpenny
Referee: A. Kingscott (Derby)

1897-98 Amateur Cup

First Round

Chesham Generals vs 3rd Grenadier Guards	4-1
Cheshunt vs Marlow	1-2
2nd Coldstream Guards vs Street	3-0
Darlington vs Hunslet	4-1
Ipswich Town vs Uxbridge	1-2
Kirkley vs Casuals	1-1
Maidenhead vs Ealing	3-1
Middlesbrough vs Leadgate Park	4-0
Old Etonians walk-over (Grays United were disqualified)	
Old Malvernians vs Kings Lynn	3-0
Old Westminsters vs Wycombe Wanderers	0-5

Sheffield vs Crook Town	2-1
Stockton vs Rutherford College	3-1
Thornaby vs Bishop Auckland	2-0
Thornaby Utopians vs Tow Law	1-0
Weybridge vs Faversham	5-0

First Round Replay

Casuals vs Kirkley	6-1

Second Round

Casuals vs Old Etonians	0-0
Chesham Generals vs Marlow	4-2
Darlington vs Stockton	1-0
Maidenhead vs Old Malvernians	2-3
Middlesbrough vs Thornaby Utopians	1-1
Sheffield vs Thornaby	1-3
Uxbridge vs Weybridge	1-0
Wycombe Wanderers vs 2nd Coldstream Guards	3-1

Second Round Replays

Old Etonians vs Casuals	1-3
Thornaby Utopians vs Middlesbrough (at Middlesbrough)	2-3

Third Round

Casuals vs Middlesbrough	0-1
Old Malvernians vs Chesham Generals	4-2
Thornaby vs Darlington	3-1
Uxbridge vs Wycombe Wanderers	1-1

Third Round Replay

Wycombe Wanderers vs Uxbridge	2-4

Semi-Finals

Middlesbrough vs Thornaby (at Brotton)	2-1
Uxbridge vs Old Malvernians (at Marlow)	1-0

Final

Uxbridge vs Middlesbrough (at Crystal Palace 23 April 1898)	0-2

Attendance: 1,500

Middlesbrough: Smith, Moore, Piercy, Allport, Jackson, Nelmes, Frost, Bishop, Kempley, Longstaff, Wanless
Scorers: Kempley, Frost*
* Some reports attribute the second goal to Bishop
Uxbridge: Gumbrell, Gayland, Skinner, Brown, Benstead, Jacobs, A. Woodbridge, Hickman, Browning, Knight, E. Woodbridge
Referee: J. Adams (Birmingham)

1898-99 Amateur Cup

First Round

Bishop Auckland vs Darlington	0-3
Chesham Generals vs Marlow	3-3
Cheshunt walk-over (Weymouth scratched)	
Devizes vs Aylesbury United	1-1
Maidenhead vs Leytonstone	4-3
Middlesbrough vs Thornaby Utopians	0-1
Old Malvernians vs Eastbourne	5-1
Old Weymouthians vs Grimsby All Saints	1-4
Royal Artillery (Portsmouth) vs Kirkley	4-0
Richmond Association vs Casuals	1-2
South Bank vs Rutherford College	5-1
Thornaby vs Mickley	0-1
Tow Law vs Stockton	2-4
(at Stockton)	
Uxbridge vs Harwich & Parkeston	1-1
Whitby vs Crook Town	9-0
Wycombe Wanderers vs Brentford	2-3

First Round Replays

Aylesbury United vs Devizes	1-0
Harwich & Parkeston vs Uxbridge	1-0
Marlow vs Chesham Generals	1-1

First Round Second Replay

Chesham Generals vs Marlow	1-8
(at Wycombe)	

Second Round

Aylesbury United vs Old Malvernians	2-3
Grimsby All Saints walk-over (Brentford scratched)	
Casuals vs Cheshunt	4-0
Darlington vs South Bank	4-1
Harwich & Parkeston vs Maidenhead	3-0
Mickley vs Whitby	1-3
Royal Artillery (Portsmouth) vs Marlow	2-0
Thornaby Utopians vs Stockton	0-3

Second Round Replay

Cheshunt vs Casuals	2-0
(after protest)	

Third Round

Grimsby All Saints vs Darlington	1-0
Harwich & Parkeston vs Royal Artillery (Portsmouth)	1-3*
* Royal Artillery (Portsmouth) were later disqualified and Harwich & Parkeston reinstated	

Semi-Finals

Harwich & Parkeston vs Grimsby All Saints	2-1
(at Ipswich)	
Stockton vs Old Malvernians	2-0
(at Darlington)	

Final

Stockton vs Harwich & Parkeston	1-0
(at Linthorpe Road, Middlesbrough 25 March 1899)	

Attendance: 7,000

Stockton: Fall, W. Shaw, Wilson, Brannen, Baker, Monteith, R. Shaw, Chatt, Byron, Fairbairn, Lakey
Scorer: Fairbairn
Harwich & Parkeston: Keith, Bacon, Howard, Ingham, Garton, Whitehead, Garland, Eley, Harwood, Taylor, Snodgrass
Referee: F. Bye (Sheffield)

1899-1900 Amateur Cup

First Round

Bishop Auckland vs Darlington St. Augustine's	6-0
Colchester Town vs Ealing	3-2
Grimsby All Saints vs Sheffield	5-1
Harwich & Parkeston vs West Croydon	0-0
Horsham vs Cheshunt	4-7
Hunslet vs Thornaby	4-0
Kings Lynn vs Thornaby Utopians	3-0
Kirkley vs Leytonstone	2-4
Liverpool Casuals walk-over (Mickley scratched)	
Lowestoft Town vs Richmond Association	6-1
Old Etonians vs Weymouth	8-0
Old Malvernians vs Weybridge	7-2
South Bank vs Crook Town	0-2
Tow Law vs Stockton	0-2
(at Stockton)	
Whitby vs Darlington	1-5
Wycombe Wanderers vs Marlow	1-1

First Round Replays

Marlow vs Wycombe Wanderers	1-0
West Croydon walk-over Harwich & Parkeston	
The tie was awarded to West Croydon	

Second Round

Colchester Town vs Old Malvernians	3-2*, 3-3
* match abandoned	
Grimsby All Saints vs Hunslet	3-2
Kings Lynn walk-over (Crook Town scratched)	
Leytonstone vs Old Etonians	2-0
Liverpool Casuals vs Darlington	2-4

Lowestoft Town vs Cheshunt — 9-0
Marlow vs West Croydon — 3-0
Stockton vs Bishop Auckland — 2-4

Second Round Replay

Old Malvernians vs Colchester Town — 9-2

Third Round

Bishop Auckland vs Kings Lynn — 4-1
Darlington vs Grimsby All Saints — 6-2
Lowestoft Town vs Leytonstone — 9-0
Marlow vs Old Malvernians — 3-1

Semi-Finals

Darlington vs Bishop Auckland — 2-2
(at Stockton)
Lowestoft Town vs Marlow — 1-0
(at Ilford)

Semi-Final Replay

Bishop Auckland vs Darlington — 2-0
(at Stockton)

Final

Bishop Auckland vs Lowestoft Town — 5-1
(at Leicester 31 March 1900)
Attendance: 1,000

Bishop Auckland: Proud, Bousfield, Condon, Ord, Thomas, Pennington, J. Marshall, Allan, T. Marshall, L. Marshall, Crawford
Scorers: Allan, T. Marshall 2, J. Marshall, Ord
Lowestoft Town: Ayres, Timoney, Mewis, Marr, Royal, Beatton, Crews, Cole, Allen, Baker, Wilkins
Scorer: Baker
Referee: A. Green (West Bromwich)

1900-01 Amateur Cup

First Round

Bedminster St. Francis vs Eastbourne — 3-2
Bishop Auckland vs Loughborough Corinthians — 3-1
Crook Town vs Stockton — 2-1
Crouch End Vampires vs Old Malvernians — 3-5
Darlington vs Stockton St. John's — 2-0
Darlington St. Augustine's vs South Bank — 2-0
Ipswich Town vs Old Etonians — 2-6
Kings Lynn vs Lowestoft Town — 2-1
Marlow vs Harwich & Parkeston — 1-2
Scarborough vs Grimsby All Saints — 1-3
Sheffield vs Mickley — 0-2

Slough vs Ealing — 0-2
Surbiton Hill vs Great Yarmouth — 4-1
Tow Law vs Hunslet — 1-6
(at Hunslet)
Wycombe Wanderers vs Richmond Association — 4-0
Thornaby Utopians — bye

Second Round

Bishop Auckland vs Darlington St. Augustine's — 2-1
Crook Town vs Mickley — 5-0
Darlington vs Grimsby All Saints — 1-0
Ealing vs Wycombe Wanderers — 5-2
Harwich & Parkeston vs Old Etonians — 4-1
Kings Lynn vs Bedminster St. Francis — 4-2
Old Malvernians vs Surbiton Hill — 4-3
Thornaby Utopians vs Hunslet — 1-3

Third Round

Darlington vs Crook Town — 0-2
Hunslet vs Bishop Auckland — 0-3
Kings Lynn vs Harwich & Parkeston — 3-1
Old Malvernians vs Ealing — 0-3

Semi-Finals

Crook Town vs Bishop Auckland — 2-0
(at Darlington)
Kings Lynn vs Ealing — 1-0
(at Norwich)

Final

Kings Lynn vs Crook Town — 1-1
(at Dovercourt, Essex 6 April 1901)
Attendance: 4,000

Crook Town: Nattrass, Ward, Rule, Law, Rippon, Hammill, Lear, Creasor, Iley, Dargue, Harwood
Scorer: Iley
Kings Lynn: Gay, Horlock, Girton, Reed, Stevens, Sporne, Orviss, Holroyd, MacDonald, Horsley, Smith
Scorer: MacDonald
Referee: F.H. King (London)

Final Replay

Crook Town vs Kings Lynn — 3-0
(at Ipswich 13 April 1901)
Attendance: 1,500

Crook Town: Nattrass, Ward, Rule, Law, Rippon, Hammill, Lear, Creasor, Iley, Harwood, Dargue
Scorers: Harwood, Rippon, Hammill
Kings Lynn: Gay, Sporne, Girton, Reed, Stevens, Haylock, Orviss, Holroyd, MacDonald, Horsley, Smith
Referee: F.H. King (London)

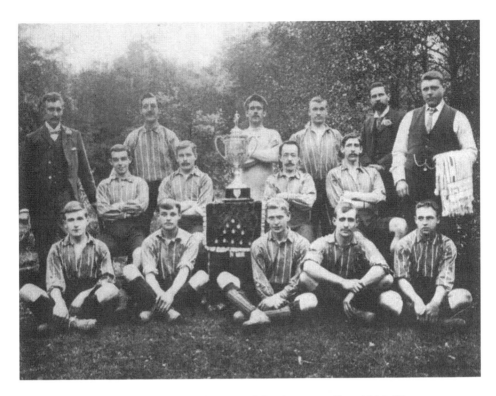

Crook Town F.C., winners of the Amateur Cup 1900-01.

back row: W. Dryburgh (Treasurer), C. Ward, J. Nattrass, I. Rule, T. Raine (President), S. Dennison (Trainer); *middle row*: C. Law, N. Rippon (Secretary), T. Hammell (Captain), W. Iley; *front row*: W. Lear, A. Creasor, R. Iley, G. Dargue, A. Harwood

1901-02 Amateur Cup

First Round

Bishop Auckland vs Hunslet	5-1
Bury Athenaeum vs Scarborough	5-1
Civil Service vs Ilford	1-2
Crook Town vs Derby Hills Ivanhoe	0-3
Darlington St. Augustine's vs West Hartlepool	2-0
Darlington St. Hilda's vs Darlington	3-1
Kings Lynn vs Kirkley	2-0
Marlow vs Oxford City	3-4
New Brompton Amateurs vs Old Etonians	4-3
Old Malvernians vs Southall	5-1
Sheffield vs Stanley United	7-3
(at Owlerton)	
Shoreham vs Ealing	1-3
South Bank vs Tow Law	4-1
Stockton vs Stockton St. John's	0-1
Surbiton Hill vs Ipswich Town	1-1
Whiteheads (Weymouth) vs Lowestoft Town	3-1

First Round Replay

Ipswich Town vs Surbiton Hill	3-0

Second Round

Bishop Auckland vs Stockton St. John's	5-2
Bury Athenaeum vs Derby Hills Ivanhoe	1-3
Darlington St. Hilda's vs Sheffield	3-1
Ealing vs Ipswich Town	1-2
Ilford vs Oxford City	1-0
New Brompton Amateurs vs Whiteheads (Weymouth)	0-1
Old Malvernians vs Kings Lynn	3-0
South Bank vs Darlington St. Augustine's	4-3

Third Round

Derby Hills Ivanhoe vs Bishop Auckland	1-4
(at the Baseball Ground)	
Ilford vs Whiteheads (Weymouth)	1-1
Old Malvernians vs Ipswich Town	10-0
South Bank vs Darlington St. Hilda's	4-2

Third Round Replay

Whiteheads (Weymouth) vs Ilford   3-6

Semi-Finals

Bishop Auckland vs South Bank   5-2
(at Darlington)
Old Malvernians vs Ilford   6-4
(at Tottenham)

Final

Bishop Auckland vs Old Malvernians   1-5
(at Headingley, Leeds 12 April 1902)
Attendance: 1,000

Old Malvernians: Tuff, Simpson-Hayward, Ransome, Todd, Canny, Simpson, Day, Corbett, R. Foster, Graeme
Scorers: Corbett, R. Foster 2, Graeme, Day
Bishop Auckland: Proud, Harwood, Condon, Jim Marshall, Thomas, T. Marshall, Joe Marshall, Allan, Newton, Wood, Crawford
Scorer: Wood
Referee: F. Bye (Sheffield)

1902-03 Amateur Cup

First Round

Army Service Corps vs Civil Service	2-2
Bedminster St. Francis vs Cheshunt	1-4
Bishop Auckland vs Darlington	3-0
Darlington St. Augustine's vs Stockton	1-4
Derby Hills Ivanhoe vs Leadgate Park	1-0
Ealing vs Kirkley	1-0
Ilford vs New Brompton Amateurs	1-0
Kimberley St. John's vs Darlington St. Hilda's	0-2
Lowestoft Town vs Poole	2-0
Old Xaverians vs South Bank	2-3
Oxford City vs Woodford	3-0
Sheffield vs Scarborough	3-0
Southall vs Chesham Generals	5-1
Tow Law vs Crook Town	0-1
Tunbridge Wells vs Marlow	2-1
West Hartlepool vs Stockton St. John's	1-0

First Round Replay

Civil Service vs Army Service Corps   2-0

Second Round

Bishop Auckland vs South Bank	6-1
Cheshunt vs Lowestoft Town	2-3
Civil Service vs Southall	8-1
Darlington St. Hilda's vs Stockton	1-2

Ealing vs Tunbridge Wells	4-3
Ilford vs Oxford City	0-1
Sheffield vs Crook Town	0-1
West Hartlepool vs Derby Hills Ivanhoe	2-1

Third Round

Bishop Auckland vs Crook Town	7-0
Civil Service vs Oxford City	1-1
Ealing vs Lowestoft Town	1-5
West Hartlepool vs Stockton	0-4

Third Round Replay

Oxford City vs Civil Service   3-1

Semi-Finals

Lowestoft Town vs Oxford City   1-1
(at Ipswich)
Stockton vs Bishop Auckland   3-1
(at Darlington)

Semi-Final Replay

Oxford City vs Lowestoft Town   4-0
(at Slough)

Final

Oxford City vs Stockton   0-0
(at Reading 28 March 1903)
Attendance: 4,000

Stockton: Lowe, Starling, King, Rutter, Bell, Hassett, Dunn, Payne, Morgan, Freeland, Blake
Oxford City: Selby, Witherington, H. Smith, Craddock, Ashworth, Dickinson, Draper, Foster, Blackburn, W. Smith, Arnett
Referee: A.C. Farrant (Bristol)

Final Replay

Stockton vs Oxford City   1-0
(at Feethams Ground, Darlington 4 April 1903)
Attendance: 7,000

Stockton: Lowe, Starling, King, Rutter, Bell, Hassett, Dunn, Payne, Morgan, Freeland, Blake
Scorer: Morgan
Oxford City: Selby, Witherington, H. Smith, Craddock, Ashworth, Egley, Draper, Foster, Blackburn, W. Smith, Arnett
Referee: A.C. Farrant (Bristol)

1903-04 Amateur Cup

First Round

Cheshunt vs Civil Service	2-1
Darlington St. Augustine's vs Rutherford College	1-1
Ealing vs Southall	4-0
Grangetown Athletic vs Crook Town	1-0
Ilford vs Kings Lynn	5-0*, 5-1
Liverpool Casuals vs Loughborough Corinthians	1-8
(at Loughborough)	
Maidenhead Norfolkians vs Tunbridge Wells	5-1*, 2-2
Norwich City vs Lowestoft Town	3-0
Paulton Amateurs vs Oxford City	2-2
Poole vs Whiteheads (Weymouth)	0-2
Sheffield vs Hessle	5-3
South Bank vs Bishop Auckland	0-2
Stockton vs Saltburn	3-1
West Hampstead vs Croydon	6-0
West Hartlepool vs Darlington	2-4
(at Darlington)	
York City St. Clements vs Scarborough	0-2

* matches abandoned

First Round Replays

Oxford City vs Paulton Amateurs	2-0
Rutherford College vs Darlington St. Augustine's	1-2
Tunbridge Wells vs Maidenhead Norfolkians	2-1

Second Round

Cheshunt vs Oxford City	1-1
Darlington vs Bishop Auckland	1-4
Darlington St. Augustine's vs Scarborough	3-1
Loughborough Corinthians vs Sheffield	1-4
Norwich City vs Ilford	3-1
Stockton vs Grangetown Athletic	5-2
Tunbridge Wells vs Ealing	3-3
Whiteheads (Weymouth) vs West Hampstead	4-2

Second Round Replays

Ealing vs Tunbridge Wells	4-0
Oxford City vs Cheshunt	4-5

Third Round

Bishop Auckland vs Stockton	4-1
Ealing vs Norwich City	0-0
Sheffield vs Darlington St. Augustine's	7-0
Whiteheads (Weymouth) vs Cheshunt	2-2

Third Round Replays

Cheshunt vs Whiteheads (Weymouth)	4-0
Norwich City vs Ealing	1-2

Semi-Finals

Ealing vs Cheshunt	2-0
(at Slough)	
Sheffield vs Bishop Auckland	5-2
(at Derby)	

Final

Sheffield vs Ealing	3-1
(at Bradford 4 April 1904)	

Attendance: 4,000

Sheffield: Bolsover, Chambers, Milne, Green, Potts, Frost, Silvester, Bedford, G. Hoyland, J. Hoyland, Forsdyke
Scorers: J. Hoyland, Bedford, Milne (penalty)
Ealing: Findlay, Blackburn, Fox, Wood, Mitchell, Pryce, Grice, Hebden, Doll, Powell, Rogers
Scorer: Hebden
Referee: A.G. Hines (Nottingham)

1904-05 Amateur Cup

First Round

Bishop Auckland vs Leadgate Park	1-0
Cheshunt vs Southend Athletic	2-2
Civil Service vs Chesham Town	3-0
Clapton vs Ipswich Town	9-0
Darlington vs Stockton	3-0
Darlington St. Augustine's walk-over (Rutherford College withdrew)	
Derby Hills Ivanhoe vs Notts Jardines	1-3
Hanwell vs Ealing	1-6
Ilford walk-over (Norwich City scratched)	
Northern Nomads vs Old Xaverians	4-1*

* a replay was ordered after a protest

Oxford City vs Whiteheads (Weymouth)	2-1
Service Battalion Royal Engineers vs Townley Park	3-3
Sheffield Grasshoppers vs Sheffield	2-1
Shepherds Bush vs Tunbridge Wells	5-1
South Bank vs Ripon United	12-0
West Hartlepool vs Grangetown Athletic	2-1

First Round Replays

Old Xaverians walk-over (Northern Nomads scratched)	
Southend Athletic vs Cheshunt	6-0
Townley Park vs Service Battalion Royal Engineers	0-2

Second Round

Bishop Auckland vs Sheffield Grasshoppers	5-1
Civil Service vs Ilford	1-3
Darlington vs South Bank	6-2
Darlington St. Augustine's vs Old Xaverians	6-1

Ealing vs Oxford City	1-1
Notts Jardines vs West Hartlepool	1-4
(at City Ground)	
Shepherds Bush vs Service Battalion Royal Engineers	0-1
Southend Athletic vs Clapton	0-1

Second Round Replay

| Oxford City vs Ealing | 1-0 |

Third Round

Bishop Auckland vs Darlington	1-0
Clapton vs Oxford City	3-0
Darlington St. Augustine's vs West Hartlepool	0-1
Ilford vs Service Battalion Royal Engineers	5-1

Semi-Finals

Clapton vs Ilford	2-1
(at Tottenham)	
West Hartlepool vs Bishop Auckland	2-1
(at Stockton)	

Final

| Clapton vs West Hartlepool | 2-3 |
| (at Shepherds Bush 8 April 1905) | |

Attendance: 4,000

Clapton: Wilding, Bayley, Langhorne, Milton, P. Farnfield, Hollis, Folks, Brown, Purnell, H. Farnfield, A. Farnfield
Scorers: Purnell 2
West Hartlepool: Bainbridge, T. Hegarty, R. Hegarty, Black, Hyslop, Stokes, Larkin, Fairweather, Robinson, Trechmann, Hodgson
Scorers: Trechmann 2, T. Hegarty
Referee: A. Kingscott (Derby)

1905-06 Amateur Cup

First Round

Bishop Auckland vs Darlington St. Augustine's	5-3
Blackburn Crosshill vs Sheffield Grasshoppers	5-1
Clapton vs Civil Service	3-0
Darlington vs South Bank	0-0
Ealing vs Gosport United	2-1
Grangetown Athletic vs West Hartlepool	1-1
2nd Grenadier Guards vs Eastbourne	1-1
Ilford vs Cheshunt	1-3
New Crusaders vs Townley Park	6-2
Northern Nomads vs Notts Jardines	2-1
Old Xaverians vs Scarborough	1-2
(at Scarborough)	
Oxford City vs Dulwich Hamlet	4-0

Romford vs Ipswich Town	4-2
Sheffield vs Bingley	7-1
Stockton vs Shildon Athletic	5-1
Uxbridge vs Tunbridge Wells	4-2

First Round Replay

Eastbourne vs 2nd Grenadier Guards	1-0
South Bank vs Darlington	2-1
West Hartlepool vs Grangetown Athletic	0-2

Second Round

Bishop Auckland vs Northern Nomads	3-1
Blackburn Crosshill vs Grangetown Athletic	3-3
Cheshunt vs Clapton	1-1
Ealing vs New Crusaders	1-5
Romford vs Eastbourne	6-3
Scarborough vs South Bank	2-4
Sheffield vs Stockton	0-6
Uxbridge vs Oxford City	1-1

Second Round Replays

Clapton vs Cheshunt	0-1
Grangetown Athletic vs Blackburn Crosshill	4-0
Oxford City vs Uxbridge	5-1

Third Round

Grangetown Athletic vs Stockton	1-5
Oxford City vs Cheshunt	4-1
Romford vs New Crusaders	0-0
South Bank vs Bishop Auckland	2-2

Third Round Replays

| Bishop Auckland vs South Bank | 2-1 |
| New Crusaders vs Romford | 1-1 |

Third Round Second Replay

| New Crusaders vs Romford | 4-1 |
| (at Stamford Bridge) | |

Semi-Finals

Bishop Auckland vs Stockton	0-0
(at Darlington)	
Oxford City vs New Crusaders	4-2
(at Reading	

Semi-Final Replay

| Bishop Auckland vs Stockton | 1-0 |
| (at Darlington) | |

Final

Bishop Auckland vs Oxford City	0-3

(at Stockton 24 March 1906)

Attendance: 5,000

Oxford City: Keates, Scothorn, Blackburn, Organ, Smith, Bumpus, Draper, Dickinson, Tabernacle, Hodges, Davis
Scorers: Hodges, Tabernacle 2
Bishop Auckland: Proud, Ord, Campbell, Kirby, Robinson, Parker, Crawford, Douglas, Hopper, Charnock, Blaylock
Referee: A. Hale

1906-07 Amateur Cup

First Round

Barnet Alston Works Athletic vs Cheshunt	4-0
Bishop Auckland vs Loughborough Corinthians	4-1
Civil Service vs Ealing	3-2
Eastbourne vs Clapton	1-2
Ilford vs New Crusaders	1-1
Kings Lynn vs Dulwich Hamlet	1-3
2nd Lincoln Regiment vs Wanstead	5-0
New Brighton Tower Amateurs vs Northern Nomads	1-2
Redhill vs Oxford City	1-4
Romanby (Northallerton) vs Rotherham Amateurs	0-5
Saltburn vs Grangetown Athletic	1-0*

* Grangetown Athletic were reinstated after Saltburn were disqualified

Sheffield vs Darlington	4-2
Stanley United vs Notts Jardines	1-1
Stockton vs Blackburn Crosshill	8-1
West Hartlepool vs South Bank	1-1
Wycombe Wanderers vs 2nd Grenadier Guards	3-5

First Round Replays

New Crusaders vs Ilford	4-1
Notts Jardines vs Stanley United	2-3
South Bank vs West Hartlepool	3-1

Second Round

Bishop Auckland vs Grangetown Athletic	5-2
Clapton vs 2nd Grenadier Guards	1-0
Dulwich Hamlet vs Civil Service	0-5
2nd Lincoln Regiment vs Barnet Alston Works Athletic	3-2
New Crusaders vs Oxford City	0-1
Northern Nomads vs South Bank	0-0
Sheffield vs Rotherham Amateurs	1-2
Stockton vs Stanley United	2-0

Second Round Replay

South Bank vs Northern Nomads	4-1

Third Round

Civil Service vs 2nd Lincoln Regiment	3-1

(at Stamford Bridge)

Clapton vs Oxford City	1-0
South Bank vs Bishop Auckland	1-1
Stockton vs Rotherham Amateurs	1-1

Third Round Replays

Bishop Auckland vs South Bank	0-2
Rotherham Amateurs vs Stockton	0-1

Semi-Finals

Clapton vs Civil Service	1-0

(at Gunnersbury Avenue, Ealing)

Stockton vs South Bank	1-0

(at Bishop Auckland)

Final

Clapton vs Stockton	2-1

(at Stamford Bridge, London 30 March 1907)

Attendance: 6,000

Clapton: Wilding, Bayley, Ewan, Parkinson, Randall, Olley, Eastwood, Russell, Rance, Purnell, Harvey
Scorers: Russell, Rance
Stockton: Gray, Charlton, Chapman, Prosser, Bell, Hassett, Williamson, Featherstone, Chambers, Freeland, Marwood
Scorer: Chambers
Referee: J.T. Ibbotson (Derby)

1907-08 Amateur Cup

First Round

Apsley vs 1st Royal Scots Guards	1-1
Atherstone Town vs Notts Magdala	4-1
Bromley vs West Norwood	2-2
Clapton vs 4th Battalion King's Royal Rifles	4-1
Custom House vs South Weald	1-0
Darlington vs West Auckland	0-2
Depot Battalion Royal Engineers vs Barnet Alston	0-0

(at Finchley)

Dulwich Hamlet vs 1st Scots Guards	0-0
2nd Grenadier Guards vs Guildford	2-2
Guards Depot vs Deptford Invicta	0-2
Ilford vs Romford	3-2
Kings Lynn vs Kirkley	3-0
Leytonstone vs Upton Park	5-1
2nd Lincolnshire Regiment vs Dorking	0-3
London Caledonians vs Nunhead	0-3
Lowestoft Town vs Stamford Town	0-0
Manchester University vs Northern Nomads	1-2

Marlow vs Maidenhead Norfolkians	1-4
Radstock Town vs Whiteheads (Weymouth)	4-1
Reading Amateurs vs Wycombe Wanderers	0-0
Reading Grovelands vs Oxford City	2-4
Saltburn vs Grangetown Athletic	1-1
Scarborough vs Spennymoor United	0-1
Sheffield vs Blackburn Crosshill	0-0
Shepherds Bush vs Chesham Town	2-0
Sneinton vs Buxton	2-1
South Bank vs Crook Town	2-1
Stockton vs Stanley United	1-1
Wantage Town vs Paulton Amateurs	1-2
West Hartlepool vs Bishop Auckland	0-3
Windsor & Eton vs Summerstown	2-0
Worthing vs Godalming	5-0

First Round Replays

Barnet Alton vs Depot Battalion Royal Engineers	2-4
Blackburn Crosshill vs Sheffield	1-0
Grangetown Athletic vs Saltburn	2-0
Guildford vs 2nd Grenadier Guards	0-2
1st Royal Scots Guards vs Apsley	3-0
1st Scots Guards vs Dulwich Hamlet	2-2
Stamford Town vs Lowestoft Town	3-0
Stanley United vs Stockton	0-1
West Norwood vs Bromley	0-2
Wycombe Wanderers vs Reading Amateurs	5-3

First Round Second Replay

Dulwich Hamlet vs 1st Scots Guards	3-4
(at Dulwich)	

Second Round

Atherstone Town vs Sneinton	3-0
Custom House vs Kings Lynn	4-1
Depot Battalion Royal Engineers vs 1st Scots Guards	4-0
Deptford Invicta vs Nunhead	2-1
Dorking vs Worthing	1-4
Grangetown Athletic vs West Auckland	0-2
2nd Grenadier Guards vs Shepherds Bush	2-2
Ilford vs Stamford Town	8-0
Leytonstone vs Clapton	1-1
Maidenhead Norfolkians vs Wycombe Wanderers	6-0
Oxford City vs Windsor & Eton	5-0
Paulton Amateurs vs Radstock Town	4-1
1st Royal Scots Guards vs Bromley	2-0
South Park vs Northern Nomads	1-1
Spennymoor United vs Bishop Auckland	1-1
Stockton vs Blackburn Crosshill	8-0

Second Round Replays

Bishop Auckland vs Spennymoor United	3-1
Clapton vs Leytonstone	2-0

Northern Nomads vs South Bank	4-2
Shepherds Bush vs 2nd Grenadier Guards	1-0

Third Round

Bishop Auckland vs West Auckland	3-1
Clapton vs 1st Royal Scots Guards	2-3
Depot Battalion Royal Engineers vs Shepherds Bush	3-0
Maidenhead Norfolkians vs Ilford	2-6
Oxford City vs Deptford Invicta	6-2
Paulton Amateurs vs Atherstone Town	2-2
Stockton vs Northern Nomads	3-1
Worthing vs Custom House	6-0

Third Round Replay

Atherstone Town vs Paulton Amateurs	1-0

Fourth Round

Atherstone Town vs Oxford City	2-1
Depot Battalion Royal Engineers vs Worthing	1-1
Ilford vs 1st Royal Scots Guards	1-1
Stockton vs Bishop Auckland	5-3

Fourth Round Replays

1st Royal Scots Guards vs Ilford	1-0
Worthing vs Depot Battalion Royal Engineers	0-1

Semi-Finals

Depot Battalion Royal Engineers vs 1st Royal Scots Guards (at Ramsgate)	2-0
Stockton vs Atherstone Town (at Darlington)	3-0

Final

Stockton vs Depot Battalion Royal Engineers (at Bishop Auckland 11 April 1908)	1-2

Attendance: 8,000

Depot Battalion Royal Engineers: Aston, Stanton, May, Shallcross, Webber, Daffern, Lowe, Keir, Pearson, Shephard, Hawthorne

Scorers: Keir, Pearson

Stockton: Gray, Bell, Chapman, Prosser, Charlton, Hassett, Williamson, Chambers, Henderson, Freeland, Lowther

Scorer: Lowther

Referee: J.H. Pearson (Cheshire)

1908-09 Amateur Cup

First Round

Barking vs Chelmsford	4-1
Bournville Athletic vs Atherstone Town	1-5
Clapton vs Newportonians	4-0
Crook Town vs West Auckland	0-2
Darlington St. Augustine's vs Bishop Auckland	4-2
Depot Battalion Royal Engineers vs West Norwood	1-0
Deptford Invicta vs Bromley	2-2
Dulwich Hamlet vs Foots Cray	4-0
Great Yarmouth Town vs Chatteris Engineers	2-1
Hereford City vs Clevedon	1-2
Ilford vs Romford	4-4
Kings Lynn vs Kirkley	2-0
4th Battalion King's Royal Rifles vs Ware	9-4
Leicestershire Regiment vs Woking	2-1
Leytonstone vs Barnet Alston Athletic	4-0
London Caledonians vs Tufnell Park	1-2
Luton Clarence vs Chesham Town	2-4
Metrogas vs Nunhead	0-7
New Brighton Tower Amateurs vs Preston Winckley	1-3
Northern Nomads vs Sheffield	3-1
Oxford City vs Uxbridge	4-1
Poole vs 2nd Scottish Rifles	0-2
Reading Amateurs vs Caversham Rovers	1-4
Redhill vs Shepherds Bush	0-1
South Bank vs West Hartlepool Expansion	4-1
South Nottingham vs Sneinton	3-0
Stanley United vs Leadgate Park	4-2
Stockton vs Eston United	1-2
Upton Park vs 2nd Grenadier Guards	2-1
West Hartlepool vs Scarborough	8-2
Whiteheads (Weymouth) vs Radstock Town	4-0*
Worthing vs Southwick	3-1

* match abandoned but awarded to Whiteheads

First Round Replays

Bromley vs Deptford Invicta	4-1
Romford vs Ilford	0-1

Second Round

Atherstone Town vs South Nottingham	2-0
Barking vs Upton Park	3-0
Chesham Town vs Caversham Rovers	5-1
Clevedon vs Whiteheads (Weymouth)	3-0
Darlington St. Augustine's vs Northern Nomads	2-0†
Depot Battalion Royal Engineers vs Bromley	0-0
Dulwich Hamlet vs Leicestershire Regiment	3-1
Eston United vs Preston Winckley	3-0
Great Yarmouth Town vs Clapton	0-1
Kings Lynn vs Leytonstone	2-2
4th Battalion King's Royal Rifles vs Ilford	1-1
Nunhead vs Worthing	2-0
2nd Scottish Rifles vs Shepherds Bush	2-1
Tufnell Park vs Oxford City	3-2
West Auckland vs Stanley United	4-0†
West Hartlepool vs South Bank	1-4

† a replay was ordered after a protest

Second Round Replays

Bromley vs Depot Battalion Royal Engineers	2-0
Ilford vs 4th Battalion King's Royal Rifles	5-2
Leytonstone vs Kings Lynn	2-1
Northern Nomads vs Darlington St. Augustine's	2-2
Stanley United vs West Auckland	0-2

Second Round Second Replay

Darlington St. Augustine's vs Northern Nomads (at York)	1-2

Third Round

Bromley vs Ilford	4-2
Chesham Town vs Dulwich Hamlet (at Dulwich)	0-2
Clapton vs Tufnell Park	5-1
Clevedon vs Barking	1-2
Eston United vs West Auckland	4-2
Leytonstone vs Nunhead	2-1
2nd Scottish Rifles vs Atherstone Town	2-2
South Bank vs Northern Nomads	1-0

Third Round Replay

Atherstone Town vs 2nd Scottish Rifles	3-1

Fourth Round

Atherstone Town vs Barking	6-1
Dulwich Hamlet vs Bromley	3-0
Leytonstone vs Clapton	1-8
South Bank vs Eston United	1-2

Semi-Finals

Clapton vs Atherstone Town (at Ilford)	3-0
Eston United vs Dulwich Hamlet (at Darlington)	2-1

Final

Clapton vs Eston United   6-0
(at Ilford 17 April 1909)

Attendance: 5,000

Clapton: Jackson, Bayley, Duce, Parkinson, Rist, Olley,
Attwood, Purnell, Rance, Tall, Harvey
Scorers: Attwood, Purnell 2, Rance 3
Eston United: Harrison, Vintner, Bell, Callaghan,
Housham, Bunn, Smith, Cail, Best, Ellis, Hollis
Referee: G.H. Muir (Hampshire)

1909-10 Amateur Cup

First Round

Apsley vs Luton Clarence	0-2
Atherstone Town vs Sneinton	1-1
Bournemouth vs Poole	3-0
Bromley vs South Weald	2-0
Chesham Town vs Oxford City	2-3
Clapton vs London Caledonians	3-0
Custom House vs 2nd Grenadier Guards	2-0
Depot Battalion Royal Engineers vs Woolwich Poly	2-2
Hereford City vs Welton Rovers	2-1
Hull Day Street O.B. vs Notts Jardines	2-3
Ilford vs Clove	3-0
Kingston-on-Thames vs West Norwood	1-0
Leadgate Park vs Darlington St. Augustine's	3-0
Leytonstone vs Dulwich Hamlet	3-0
New Brighton Tower Amateurs vs Scarborough	0-1
(at Scarborough)	
Newportonians vs Barking	2-5
Northern Nomads vs Rotherham Amateurs	5-0
Norwich C.E.Y.M.S. vs Kings Lynn	4-1
Nunhead vs Woking	5-4
Ramsgate Town vs Deptford Invicta	3-3
Sheffield vs Preston Winckley	5-2*
* Sheffield were disqualified	
Shepherds Bush vs Shoeburyness Garrison	2-2
South Bank vs Bishop Auckland	2-0
South Nottingham vs Basford United	4-0
Stockton vs Crook Town	4-1
Tufnell Park vs Romford	2-1†
† a replay was ordered	
Uxbridge vs Barnet Alston	0-2
West Hartlepool vs Eston United	3-2
West Hartlepool Expansion vs West Auckland	2-1
Worthing vs R.M.L.I. (Gosport)	0-4
Wycombe Wanderers vs Caversham Rovers	5-0
Redhill received a bye	

First Round Replays

Deptford Invicta vs Ramsgate Town	4-1

Shoeburyness Garrison vs Shepherds Bush	2-2
Sneinton vs Atherstone Town	3-0
Romford vs Tufnell Park	0-1
Woolwich Poly vs Depot Battalion Royal Engineers	1-5

First Round Second Replay

Shepherds Bush vs Shoeburyness Garrison	2-0
(at Plumstead)	

Second Round

Barking vs Shepherds Bush	3-0
Bournemouth vs R.M.L.I. (Gosport)	1-3
Clapton vs Ilford	1-2†
† a replay was ordered after a protest	
Custom House vs Nunhead	2-1
Deptford Invicta vs Depot Battalion Royal Engineers	1-0
Hereford City vs South Nottingham	4-2
Kingston-on-Thames vs Redhill	0-3
Leadgate Park vs South Bank	0-3
(at South Bank)	
Leytonstone vs Norwich C.E.Y.M.S.	2-0
Northern Nomads vs Scarborough	0-0
Oxford City vs Bromley	0-2
Preston Winckley vs Stockton	4-3
(at Stockton)	
Sneinton vs Notts Jardines	2-2
Tufnell Park vs Barnet Alston	1-0
West Hartlepool Expansion vs West Hartlepool	1-1
Wycombe Wanderers vs Luton Clarence	2-0

Second Round Replays

Clapton vs Ilford	2-1
Notts Jardines vs Sneinton	3-2
Scarborough vs Northern Nomads	2-0
West Hartlepool vs West Hartlepool Expansion	1-2

Third Round

Barking vs Notts Jardines	7-2
Bromley vs R.M.L.I. (Gosport)	1-2
Deptford Invicta vs Clapton	1-3
Redhill vs Custom House	1-1
Scarborough vs Preston Winckley	1-0*
* Scarborough were disqualified	
South Bank vs West Hartlepool Expansion	2-1
Tufnell Park vs Hereford City	3-1
Wycombe Wanderers vs Leytonstone	3-2

Third Round Replay

Custom House vs Redhill	1-0

Fourth Round

Barking vs Tufnell Park	1-5

Clapton vs Wycombe Wanderers	4-1
Custom House vs R.M.L.I. (Gosport)	0-2
Preston Winckley vs South Bank	0-2

Semi-Finals

R.M.L.I. (Gosport) vs Tufnell Park	4-0
(at Portsmouth)	
South Bank vs Clapton	2-1
(at Stockton)	

Final

| South Bank vs R.M.L.I. (Gosport) | 1-2 |
| (at Bishop Auckland 16 April 1910) | |

Attendance: 8,000

R.M.L.I. (Gosport): Turner, Wilkinson, Hirst, Revill, Yates, Wiseman, Exford White, Holmes, Jack, Smith
Scorers: Jack, Holmes
South Bank: Howling, Rand, Oakley, Briggs, Prest, W. Carr, Thompson, J. Carr, H. Carr, Cartwright, Jones
Scorer: Biggs
Referee: J.R. Schumacher (London)

1910-11 Amateur Cup

First Round

Army Ordnance Corps vs St. Albans City	0-2
(at St. Albans)	
Barking vs South Weald	4-3
Barnet Alston Athletic vs Kings Lynn	5-1
Bromley vs Catford Southend	1-0
Chelmsford vs South Nottingham	2-2
Chesham Town vs Shepherds Bush	1-3
Clapton vs 2nd Coldstream Guards	0-1
Darlington St. Augustine's vs Bishop Auckland	0-2
Hereford City vs Royal Engineers (Aldershot)	2-2*
Ilford vs Leytonstone	2-1
1st King's Royal Rifles vs Aylesbury United	10-1
Loughborough Corinthians vs London Caledonians	2-0
Luton Clarence vs Enfield	3-2
Northern Nomads vs Eston United	0-0
Notts Jardines vs Atherstone Town	4-0
Old Kingstonians vs Branksome Gasworks Athletic	2-1*
Preston Winckley vs Stanley United	0-4
Redhill vs Caversham Rovers	3-1
R.M.L.I. (Gosport) vs Dulwich Hamlet	0-2
Sandbach Ramblers vs Sheffield	4-0
Scarborough vs Langley Park	3-2
Sneinton vs Norwich C.E.Y.M.S.	2-1
Southall vs Nunhead	1-2
South Bank vs Rotherham Amateurs	1-1
Southwick vs 1st North Staffs Regiment	1-3

Stockton vs West Auckland	0-0
Swindon Victoria vs Wycombe Wanderers	1-1
(at Wycombe)	
Tufnell Park vs Shoeburyness Garrison	5-2
West Norwood vs Old Wulfrunians	2-1
Woking vs Clevedon	4-3
York City vs Crook Town	1-2
Oxford City received a bye	
* matches abandoned	

First Round Replays

Branksome Gasworks Athletic vs Old Kingstonians	3-2
Eston United walk-over (Northern Nomads scratched)	
Royal Engineers (Aldershot) vs Hereford City	3-0
South Bank vs Rotherham Amateurs	0-1
South Nottingham vs Chelmsford	2-1
West Auckland vs Stockton	2-1
Wycombe Wanderers vs Swindon Victoria	2-1

Second Round

Barking vs Oxford City	4-1
Barnet Alston Athletic vs Nunhead	1-0
Branksome Gasworks Athletic walk-over (Loughborough Corinthians scatched)	
Bromley vs Tufnell Park	4-1
2nd Coldstream Guards vs Royal Engineers (Aldershot)	3-1
Ilford vs St. Albans City	2-0
Luton Clarence vs Shepherds Bush	2-1
1st North Staffs Regiment vs South Nottingham	7-1
Notts Jardines vs 1st King's Royal Rifles	1-1
Redhill vs Dulwich Hamlet	1-0
Rotherham Amateurs vs Bishop Auckland	2-1†
† a replay was ordered after a protest	
Sandbach Ramblers vs Crook Town	3-1
Sneinton vs West Norwood	3-0
Stanley United vs Scarborough	2-0
West Auckland vs Eston United	2-1
Wycombe Wanderers vs Woking	4-3

Second Round Replays

| Bishop Auckland vs Rotherham Amateurs | 4-1 |
| 1st King's Royal Rifles vs Notts Jardines | 2-1 |

Third Round

Barking vs Luton Clarence	4-3
Barnet Alston Athletic vs 1st North Staffs Regiment	5-2
Branksome Gasworks Athletic vs Ilford	0-2
Bromley vs Sneinton	6-2
2nd Coldstream Guards vs Redhill	2-0
Sandbach Ramblers vs Stanley United	2-1†
† a replay was ordered after a protest but as Stanley United were unable to raise a team, the original result stood	

| West Auckland vs Bishop Auckland | 1-4 |
| Wycombe Wanderers vs 1st King's Royal Rifles | 4-2 |

Fourth Round

Barking vs Ilford	1-2
Barnet Alston Athletic vs Bromley	0-1
Bishop Auckland vs Sandbach Ramblers	6-0
Wycombe Wanderers vs 2nd Coldstream Guards	2-3

Semi-Finals

Bishop Auckland vs Ilford	6-0
(at Stockton)	
Bromley vs 2nd Coldstream Guards	0-0
(at Redhill)	

Semi-Final Replay

| Bromley vs 2nd Coldstream Guards | 3-0 |
| (at Redhill) | |

Final

| Bromley vs Bishop Auckland | 1-0 |
| (at Herne Hill 8th April 1911) | |

Attendance: 3,000

Bromley: Wood, Peacock, Watson, McWhirter, Noall, Smith, Dilley, Noble, Kennard, Laundrey, Grayer
Scorer: Dilley
Bishop Auckland: Walton, Rudd, Ansell, Kirby, Hedley, Robinson, Wanless, Healey, Hopper, Kent, Sowerby
Referee: J. Dickerson (Hampshire)

1911-12 Amateur Cup

First Round

Apsley vs Southall	1-2
Arden vs South Nottingham	5-3
Barking vs Custom House	2-2
Barnet Alston vs London Caledonians	0-3
Basford United vs Notts Jardines	1-0
Bournemouth Gasworks Athletic vs	
2nd Wiltshire Regiment	4-3
Colchester Town vs Walthamstow Grange	2-3
Crook Town vs South Bank	1-0
Darlington St. Augustine's vs Eston United	2-5
Dulwich Hamlet vs 2nd King's Rifles	4-0
Ilford vs Great Yarmouth Town	5-3
1st King's Royal Rifles vs R.M.L.I. (Gosport)	5-1
Leytonstone vs Clapton	1-2
Luton Clarence vs Tufnell Park	2-1*
* abandoned during extra time	
Nunhead vs Catford Southend	3-1

Redhill vs Old Kingstonians	3-0
Rotherham Amateurs vs Northumberland Fusiliers	2-0
Royal Naval Depot vs 2nd Coldstream Guards	1-0
St. Albans City vs 2nd Grenadier Guards	0-2
Scarborough vs Northern Nomads	6-1
Shepherds Bush vs Wycombe Wanderers	2-0
Sherwood Foresters vs Royal Engineers (Aldershot)	2-2
Sneinton vs Oxford City	0-2
Southport Y.M.C.A. vs Sheffield	4-0
Stanley United vs Bishop Auckland	1-2
Stockton vs Grangetown Athletic	1-0
Trowbridge Town vs Cardiff Corinthians	1-2
Tunbridge Wells vs Walton-on-Thames	2-0
Waltham vs Finchley	1-0
West Norwood vs Bromley	1-4
Willington vs West Auckland	2-0
Woking vs Pokesdown	5-0

First Round Replays

Custom House vs Barking	2-4
Royal Engineers (Aldershot) vs Sherwood Foresters	3-1
Tufnell Park vs Luton Clarence	2-0

Second Round

Basford United vs Arden	2-1
Cardiff Corinthians vs Bournemouth Gasworks Athletic	0-0
Clapton vs Barking	1-2
Crook Town vs Southport Y.M.C.A.	4-0
Dulwich Hamlet vs Tunbridge Wells	2-0
Eston United vs Scarborough	7-0
2nd Grenadier Guards vs Oxford City	0-4
Ilford vs Waltham	3-1
Nunhead vs Shepherds Bush	2-1
Redhill vs Woking	1-2
Rotherham Amateurs vs Willington	2-1
Royal Engineers (Aldershot) vs 1st King' Royal Rifles	2-1
Royal Naval Depot vs Bromley	1-6
Southall vs London Caledonians	1-2†, 0-0
† match abandoned	
Stockton vs Bishop Auckland	3-1
Walthamstow Grange vs Tufnell Park	0-1

Second Round Replays

Bournemouth Gasworks Athletic vs	
Cardiff Corinthians	5-2
London Caledonians vs Southall	1-1
(at Shepherds Bush)	

Second Round Second Replay

| Southall vs London Caledonians | 1-0 |
| (at Shepherds Bush) | |

Third Round

Barking vs Oxford City	2-0
Basford United vs Tufnell Park	0-1
Bournemouth Gasworks Athletic vs Redhill	0-1
Crook Town vs Royal Engineers (Aldershot)	1-2
Ilford vs Rotherham Amateurs	1-0
Southall vs Bromley	0-2
Stockton vs Nunhead	1-1
Woking vs Eston United	2-4

Third Round Replay

Nunhead vs Stockton	1-2

Fourth Round

Eston United vs Barking	5-2
Ilford vs Royal Engineers (Aldershot)	2-2
Stockton vs Bromley	1-0
Tufnell Park vs Dulwich Hamlet	2-0

Fourth Round Replay

Royal Engineers (Aldershot) vs Ilford	3-2
(at New Cross)	

Semi-Finals

Eston United vs Tufnell Park	1-0
(at Stockton)	
Royal Engineers (Aldershot) vs Stockton	0-1
(at Clapton)	

Final

Eston United vs Stockton	1-1
(at Ayresome Park, Middlesbrough 13 April 1912)	

Attendance: 20,000

Stockton: Callaghan, Loney, Chapman, Evans, Stamper, Veitch, Bradford, Dobinson, Sutherland, Davis, Callender
Scorer: Sutherland
Eston United: Hill, Roddam, Davidson, J. Smith, Housham, O'Hara, Allan, Parsons, W. Smith, Morris, Hollis
Scorer: Parsons
Referee: G. Watson (Sunderland)

Final Replay

Stockton vs Eston United	1-0
(at Ayresome Park, Middlesbrough 18 April 1912)	

Attendance: 12,000

Stockton: Callaghan, Loney, Chapman, Evans, Stamper, Veitch, Bradford, Dobinson, Sutherland, Davis, Callender
Scorer: Sutherland
Eston United: Hill, Roddam, Davidson, J. Smith, Housham, O'Hara, Allan, Parsons, W. Smith, Morris, Hollis
Referee: G. Watson (Sunderland)

1912-13 Amateur Cup

First Round

Barking vs Cromer	1-1
Barnet & Alston vs Maidenhead Norfolkians	3-0
Bishop Auckland vs Stanley United	2-1
Bournemouth vs Royal Engineers (Aldershot)	1-2
Catford Southend vs Summerstown	2-0
Chesham Generals vs Tufnell Park	3-1
Clapton vs 2nd Durham Light Infantry	6-2
2nd Coldstream Guards vs London Caledonians	1-2
Darlington St. Augustine's vs Stockton	2-3
Dulwich Hamlet vs Woking	5-0
Enfield vs Luton Clarence	3-2
Grangetown St. Mary's vs Crook Town	1-2
Ilford vs Custom House	1-4
Kilburn vs Southall	0-5
1st King's Royal Rifles versus	
Bournemouth Gasworks Athletic	3-0
2nd Lancashire Fusiliers vs Redhill	3-2
Leytonstone vs Grays Athletic	0-1
4th Middlesex Regiment vs Sherwood Foresters	1-6
2nd Northumberland Fusiliers vs Leadgate Park	3-3
Notts Jardines vs Basford United	0-1
Nunhead vs Army Service Corps (Woolwich)	2-0
Old Kingstonians vs Bromley	0-0
Old Wulfrunians vs Netherfield Rangers	2-4
Rotherham Amateurs vs Broughton	3-1
1st Royal N. Lancashire Regiment vs R.M.L.I. (Gosport)	1-1
Shepherds Bush vs St. Albans City	2-0
Sneinton vs Oxford City	1-8
South Bank vs Eston United	3-2
Southport Y.M.C.A. vs Northern Nomads	1-7
Trowbridge Town vs Cardiff Corinthians	2-3
West Norwood vs Worthing	3-3
Willington vs Scarborough	4-2

First Round Replays

Bromley vs Old Kingstonians	2-0
Cromer vs Barking	0-2
Leadgate Park vs 2nd Northumberland Fusiliers	0-1
R.M.L.I. (Gosport) vs 1st Royal N. Lancashire Regiment	3-1
Worthing vs West Norwood	3-0

Second Round

Barking vs Custom House	2-1
Barnet & Alston vs Southall	5-3
Bishop Auckland vs Stockton	2-3
Catford Southend vs 2nd Lancashire Fusiliers	2-2
Crook Town vs South Bank	0-0
Dulwich Hamlet vs Bromley	0-1
Grays Athletic vs Clapton	0-3
1st King's Royal Rifles vs R.M.L.I. (Gosport)	1-0
London Caledonians vs Enfield	1-0

Netherfield Rangers vs Basford United	2-1
2nd Northumberland Fusiliers vs Northern Nomads	3-2
Nunhead vs Worthing	5-0
Oxford City vs Royal Engineers (Aldershot)	5-1
St. Albans City vs Tufnell Park	1-0
Sherwood Foresters vs Cardiff Corinthians	9-1
Willington vs Rotherham Amateurs	1-5

Second Round Replays

| 2nd Lancashire Fusiliers vs Catford Southend | 2-5 |
| South Bank vs Crook Town | 2-0 |

Third Round

Bromley vs Netherfield Rangers	5-2
Clapton vs Barnet & Alston	3-0
London Caledonians vs Nunhead	1-1
2nd Northumberland Fusiliers vs Catford Southend	2-1*
* abandoned during extra time	
Oxford City vs 1st King's Royal Rifles	4-1
Rotherham Amateurs vs South Bank	0-0
Sherwood Foresters vs Barking	4-0
Stockton vs St. Albans City	1-1

Third Round Replays

Catford Southend vs 2nd Northumberland Fusiliers	2-1
Nunhead vs London Caledonians	2-1
St. Albans City vs Stockton	3-2
South Bank vs Rotherham Amateurs	2-0

Fourth Round

Bromley vs St. Albans City	4-1
Clapton vs Nunhead	4-1
Oxford City vs Sherwood Foresters	3-1
South Bank vs Catford Southend	0-0

Fourth Round Replay

| Catford Southend vs South Bank | 0-3 |

Semi-Finals

Oxford City vs Clapton	2-0
(at Reading)	
South Bank vs Bromley	2-1
(at Bishop Auckland)	

Final

| Oxford City vs South Bank | 1-1 |

(at Reading 12 April 1913)

Attendance: 6,000

South Bank: Howling, Urwin, Oakley, Henry, Prest, Anderson, Carr, Clarke, Borrie, Heron, Evans
Scorer: Borrie

Oxford City: Harley, Cadwell, Ansell, Radnage, Hunt, Slatter, Draper, MacKinnon, Buckingham, Jakeman, Smith
Scorer: Buckingham
Referee: T. Laithewaite (Lancashire)

Final Replay

| South Bank vs Oxford City | 1-0 |

(at Bishop Auckland 19 April 1913)

Attendance: 7,000

South Bank: Howling, Urwin, Oakley, Henry, Prest, Anderson, Carr, Clarke, Borrie, Heron, Evans
Scorer: Carr
Oxford City: Harley, Cadwell, Ansell, Radnage, Hunt, Slatter, Draper, Berry, Buckingham, Jakeman, Smith
Referee: T. Laithewaite (Lancashire)

1913-14 Amateur Cup

First Round

Barnet & Alston vs Slough	5-0
Basford United vs Sneinton	3-1
Bishop Auckland vs Craghead United	4-1
Bromley vs Catford Southend	1-0
Broughton vs Old Xaverians	6-1
Clapton vs Great Yarmouth Town	2-1
Colchester Town vs Barking	4-2
2nd Coldstream Guards vs Aylesbury United	5-0
3rd Coldstream Guards vs Army Service Corps	1-6
Crook Town vs Willington	1-0
Darlington St. Augustine's vs South Bank	0-1
Enfield vs Shepherds Bush	1-1*
Esh Winning vs West Hartlepool St. Joseph's	2-1*
Grays Athletic vs Custom House	0-0*
Headingley vs Old Wulfrunians	3-2
1st King's Royal Rifles vs Woking	2-1
Leytonstone vs Ilford	2-1
London Caledonians vs Chesham Generals	5-0
Metrogas vs Hersham United	4-3
4th Middlesex Regiment vs Trowbridge Town	7-4
Nunhead vs Ramsgate Town	7-1
Ogden's Athletic vs Northern Nomads	1-1
Old Kingstonians vs Dulwich Hamlet	0-1
Oxford City vs Netherfield Rangers	3-1
R.A.M.C. (Aldershot) vs Portsmouth Amateurs	4-1
Rotherham Amateurs vs Hathersage	1-1
Royal Engineers (Aldershot) versus Bournemouth Gasworks Athletic	1-1*
1st Royal Welsh Fusiliers vs Cardiff Corinthians	3-3
Southall vs St. Albans City	4-0
Stockton vs Sherwood Foresters	4-3
Tufnell Park vs Luton Clarence	4-2
Tunbridge Wells vs West Norwood	0-0*

* matches abandoned during extra time

First Round Replays

Bournemouth Gasworks Athletic versus Royal Engineers (Aldershot)	2-1
Cardiff Corinthians vs 1st Royal Welsh Fusiliers	2-1
Custom House vs Grays Athletic	1-1*
* abandoned during extra time	
Hathersage vs Rotherham Amateurs	4-0
Northern Nomads vs Ogden's Athletic	4-1
Shepherds Bush vs Enfield	0-0
Tunbridge Wells vs West Norwood	4-0
West Hartlepool St. Joseph's vs Esh Winning	1-0

First Round Second Replays

Enfield vs Shepherds Bush (at Highbury)	2-1
Grays Athletic vs Custom House (at Barking)	2-1

Second Round

Bishop Auckland vs Hathersage	5-4*
* abandoned during extra time	
Bournemouth Gasworks Athletic vs Oxford City	0-1
Cardiff Corinthians vs 4th Middlesex Regiment	4-2
Clapton vs Grays Athletic	5-1
Colchester Town vs Leytonstone	1-2
2nd Coldstream Guards vs Barnet & Alston	1-2
Crook Town vs South Bank	5-1
Dulwich Hamlet vs Army Service Corps	2-0
Headingley vs Basford United	5-3
Metrogas vs Tunbridge Wells	5-1
Northern Nomads vs Broughton	1-0
Nunhead vs Bromley	0-0
R.A.M.C. (Aldershot) vs 1st King's Royal Rifles	2-0
Southall vs Enfield	4-1
Tufnell Park vs London Caledonians	3-1
West Hartlepool St. Joseph's vs Stockton	1-2

Second Round Replays

Bishop Auckland vs Hathersage	2-1
Bromley vs Nunhead	3-1

Third Round

Barnet & Alston vs Cardiff Corinthians	3-1
Bishop Auckland vs Leytonstone	5-1
Clapton vs Crook Town	3-2
Dulwich Hamlet vs Southall	4-1
Northern Nomads vs Metrogas	3-1
R.A.M.C. (Aldershot) vs Bromley	2-2
Stockton vs Oxford City	1-0
Tufnell Park vs Headingley	5-0

Third Round Replay

Bromley vs R.A.M.C. (Aldershot)	1-6

Fourth Round

Barnet & Alston vs R.A.M.C. (Aldershot)	1-3
Clapton vs Bishop Auckland	1-2
Dulwich Hamlet vs Tufnell Park	0-0
Northern Nomads vs Stockton	2-0

Fourth Round Replay

Tufnell Park vs Dulwich Hamlet	3-1

Semi-Finals

Bishop Auckland vs R.A.M.C. (Aldershot) (at Stockton)	0-0
Tufnell Park vs Northern Nomads (at Herne Hill)	0-2

Semi-Final Replay

Bishop Auckland vs R.A.M.C. (Aldershot) (at Watford)	3-1

Final

Bishop Auckland vs Northern Nomads (at Leeds 4 April 1914)	1-0

Attendance: 5,000

Bishop Auckland: North, Roe, Rudd, Hopper, Spence, Maddison, Appleby, A. Douglass, Kirby, Spence, Lunson
Scorer: Kirby
Northern Nomads: Peever, Barlow, Cunliffe, Gotobed, Porter, McKinnon, Davies, H. Douglas, Cruse, Boardman, Salt
Referee: A. Warner (Notts)

1914-15 Amateur Cup

First Round

Barnet & Alston vs Harpenden Town	3-1
Basford United vs Mapperley	4-0
Belmont Mines Athletic vs Grangetown St. Mary's	1-0
Bishop Auckland vs West Auckland Athletic	3-0
Bromley vs Summerstown	5-1
Brooms vs Darlington St. Augustine's	6-0
Catford Southend vs West Norwood	2-2*
Chelmsford vs Ilford	1-6
Clapton vs Leytonstone	2-1
Crook Town vs Willington	2-1
Grays Athletic vs Charlton Athletic	4-1
Great Yarmouth Town vs Kings Lynn	3-1

Guildford walk-over (Metrogas scratched)

Hallam vs Rotherham Amateurs	4-2*, 4-2

Hathersage received a bye

Leadgate Park vs Esh Winning	2-1*, 4-1

London Caledonians walk-over (Tufnell Park scratched)
Lowestoft Town walk-over (Cambridge Town scratched)

Luton Albion vs Luton Clarence	4-2
Netherfield Rangers vs Sneinton	8-0
Northern Nomads vs Harrowby	0-0*

Nunhead walk-over (Old Kingstonians scratched)

Oxford City vs Slough	10-0

Page Green Old Boys walk-over (Enfield scratched)

Portsmough Amateurs vs Hove	3-0
Royal Engineers (Aldershot) vs Shepherds Bush	2-4
Southall vs Swindon Victoria	3-2
South Bank vs Scarborough	1-0
Stanley United vs Pandon Temperance	4-1
Stockton vs North Skelton Swifts	4-0

Tooting walk-over (Strood scratched)

Walthamstow Grange vs Woodford Crusaders	3-2

* matches abandoned

First Round Replays

Catford Southend vs West Norwood	2-0
Harrowby vs Northern Nomads	7-1

Second Round

Barnet & Alston vs Ilford	1-2
Bishop Auckland vs Belmont Mines Athletic	4-1
Clapton vs Southall	5-1
Grays Athletic vs London Caledonians	1-3
Harrowby vs Hallam	2-1
Hathersage vs Basford United	5-1
Lowestoft Town vs Great Yarmouth Town	2-0
Luton Albion vs Nunhead	1-4
Oxford City vs Netherfield Rangers	3-2
Page Green Old Boys vs Shepherds Bush	2-0
Portsmouth Amateurs vs Guildford	3-2
South Bank vs Crook Town	4-6
Stanley United vs Leadgate Park	6-0
Stockton vs Brooms	4-1
Tooting vs Bromley	0-1
Walthamstow Grange vs Catford Southend	6-2

Third Round

Bishop Auckland vs Stanley United	3-2
Clapton vs Bromley	2-1
Hathersage vs Harrowby	1-1
Ilford vs Portsmouth Amateurs	8-0
London Caledonians vs Oxford City	2-0
Page Green Old Boys vs Lowestoft Town	2-1
Stockton vs Crook Town	2-4
Walthamstow Grange vs Nunhead	1-2

Third Round Replay

Harrowby vs Hathersage	4-0

Fourth Round

Ilford vs Harrowby	1-0
London Caledonians vs Crook Town	6-1
Nunhead vs Bishop Auckland	3-6
Page Green Old Boys vs Clapton	0-0

Fourth Round Replay

Clapton vs Page Green Old Boys	3-1

Semi-Finals

Bishop Auckland vs Ilford	2-0
(at Darlington)	
Clapton vs London Caledonians	0-0
(at Ilford)	

Semi-Final Replay

London Caledonians vs Clapton	0-1
(at Dulwich Hamlet)	

Final

Clapton vs Bishop Auckland	1-0
(at New Cross 17 April 1915)	

Attendance: 6,000

Clapton: Wood, Sharpley, Barlemeh, Ward, Prescott, Millars, Walden, Cox, Lloyd, Sherwood, Cordell
Scorer: Sherwood
Bishop Auckland: North, Roe, Rudd, Kasher, Green, Maddison, Brown, Gardner, Hopper, Fleming, Lunson
Referee: J. Holmes (Derby)

1919-20 Amateur Cup

First Round

Barnet vs Leavesden Mental Hospital	2-3
Basford United vs Boots Athletic	1-2
Belmont Avenue vs Stanley United	1-2
Bournemouth Gasworks Athletic vs Worthing	2-1
Brighton West End vs Bishop Auckland	0-3
Cardiff Corinthians vs R.A.M.C. (Aldershot)	2-1
Catford Southend vs Bromley	1-3
Charlton Athletic vs Oxford City	1-2
Cheltenham Town vs Clandown	0-2
Chesham United vs Aylesbury Town	2-0
Crook Town vs Willington	1-0
Dulwich Hamlet vs Wimbledon	9-2
Esh Winning vs West Hartlepool St. Joseph's	0-3

Grays Athletic vs London Caledonians	2-3
Guildford vs R.M.L.I. (Gosport)	3-4
Harrowby vs Old Xaverians	4-0
Ilford vs Walthamstow Grange	3-1
Langley Park vs South Bank	2-1
Leiston Works vs Kings Lynn	2-1
Leytonstone vs Clapton	3-0
Luton Clarence vs St. Albans City	4-3
Northern Nomads vs Hallam	5-2
Nunhead vs Summerstown	4-1
Ordnance (Woolwich) vs Eastbourne	3-3
Redcar vs Stockton	2-1
Rotherham Amateurs vs Hathersage	1-2
Royal Naval Depot vs West Norwood	3-2
Scarborough vs Cockfield	3-2
Shoeburyness Garrison vs G.E.R. (Romford)	0-1
Sneinton vs Netherfield Rangers	6-1
Southall vs Slough	4-2
Tufnell Park vs Wycombe Wanderers	6-2

First Round Replay

Eastbourne vs Ordnance (Woolwich)	3-2

Second Round

Bishop Auckland vs West Hartlepool St.Joseph's	2-0
Bournemouth Gasworks Athletic vs Clandown	5-0
Bromley vs Chesham United	5-0
Cardiff Corinthians vs Dulwich Hamlet	1-2
Crook Town vs Stanley United	0-1
Eastbourne vs Sneinton	0-1
Langley Park vs Scarborough	2-1
Leavesden Mental Hospital vs Southall	2-1
Leiston Works vs Nunhead	0-2
London Caledonians vs Luton Clarence	1-0
Northern Nomads vs Harrowby	2-1
Oxford City vs Boots Athletic	1-0
Redcar vs Hathersage	2-0
R.M.L.I. (Gosport) vs Ilford	1-2
Royal Naval Depot vs Leytonstone	1-3
Tufnell Park vs G.E.R. (Romford)	0-1*

* abandoned during extra time

Second Round Replay

G.E.R. (Romford) vs Tufnell Park	2-3

Third Round

Bournemouth Gasworks Athletic vs Oxford City	0-1
Dulwich Hamlet vs Bishop Auckland	5-1
Ilford vs Northern Nomads	2-2
Langley Park vs Leavesden Mental Hospital	3-1
Nunhead vs Bromley	0-2
Sneinton vs Leytonstone	1-8
Stanley United vs Redcar	5-0

Tufnell Park vs London Caledonians	1-0

Third Round Replay

Northern Nomads vs Ilford	2-1

Fourth Round

Bromley vs Langley Park	3-1
Oxford City vs Dulwich Hamlet	1-2
Stanley United vs Leytonstone	2-1
Tufnell Park vs Northern Nomads	2-1

Semi-Finals

Dulwich Hamlet vs Bromley	2-1
(at Wimbledon)	
Stanley United vs Tufnell Park	0-1
(at Bishop Auckland)	

Final

Dulwich Hamlet vs Tufnell Park	1-0
(at The Den, Millwall 17 April 1920)	

Attendance: 25,000

Dulwich Hamlet: Coleman, Pilkington, Bowker, Jonas, Sweeting, Shipway, Kail, Davis, Nicol, Fuller
Scorer: Kail
Tufnell Park: Leese, Butcher, Evans, Goodman, Read, Swayne, Fricker, Lloyd, Hannaford, Williams, Elkington
Referee: W.E. Russell (Wiltshire)

1920-21 Amateur Cup

First Round

Barking Town vs Gorleston	5-1
Barnet vs Clapton	4-0
Bromley vs Redhill	5-0
Cardiff Corinthians vs Swansea Amateurs	4-2
Cargo Fleet Ironworks vs Eston United	2-2
Crook Town vs Stockton	3-0
Enfield vs Luton Clarence	2-6
Esh Winning vs Langley Park	1-0
Gosport vs R.M.L.I. (Gosport)	2-3
Grays Athletic vs Custom House	3-5
Hathersage vs Calverley	1-1
Kings Lynn vs Eston Works Athletic	4-2
Leavesden Mental Hospital vs Chesham United	2-3
Loftus Albion vs Redcar	5-1
London Caledonians vs Leytonstone	2-1*

* abandoned during extra time

Maidenhead United vs Kingstonian	1-2
Metrogas vs Southall	4-1
Northern Nomads vs Harrowby	4-1
Nunhead vs Royal Naval Depot (Chatham)	6-2

Oxford City vs Badsey Rangers	5-0
R.A.M.C. (Aldershot) versus	
Bournemouth Gasworks Athletic	2-0
Rushden Town vs Boots Atheltic	4-2
St. Albans City vs Ilford	0-4
Scarborough vs Hornsea	3-1
Sneinton vs R.A.F. (Cranwell)	1-0
South Bank vs Grangetown St. Mary's	1-0
Stanley United vs Bishop Auckland	0-3
Swindon Victoria vs Clandown	8-0
Wealdstone vs Tufnell Park	0-0
Willington vs West Hartlepool Expansion	4-0
Wimbledon vs Dulwich Hamlet	2-1
Wycombe Wanderers vs Signal Services T.C.	3-2

First Round Replays

Calverley vs Hathersage	3-2
Eston United vs Cargo Fleet Ironworks	3-1
Leytonstone vs London Caledonians	3-1
Tufnell Park vs Wealdstone	2-1

Second Round

Bromley vs Sneinton	5-1
Cardiff Corinthians vs Barking	3-1
Chesham United vs Tufnell Park	0-2
Esh Winning vs Eston United	3-2
Kings Lynn vs Boots Athletic	3-1
Kingstonian vs Custom House	3-2
Loftus Albion vs Scarborough	3-1
Luton Clarence vs R.A.M.C. (Aldershot)	4-3
Metrogas vs Nunhead	2-0
Northern Nomads vs Calverley	3-1
Oxford City vs Leytonstone	1-2
R.M.L.I. (Gosport) vs Swindon Victoria	0-1
South Bank vs Bishop Auckland	1-2
Willington vs Crook Town	2-0
Wimbledon vs Ilford	3-2
Wycombe Wanderers vs Barnet	4-3

Third Round

Kingstonian vs Bishop Auckland	0-2
Loftus Albion vs Kings Lynn	6-0
Luton Clarence vs Esh Winning	0-1
Metrogas vs Leytonstone	1-1
Swindon Victoria vs Bromley	1-0
Tufnell Park vs Wycombe Wanderers	1-2
Willington vs Northern Nomads	1-0
Wimbledon vs Cardiff Corinthians	1-0

Third Round Replay

Leytonstone vs Metrogas	3-2

Fourth Round

Esh Winning vs Bishop Auckland	4-5
Leytonstone vs Wimbledon	1-0
Loftus Albion vs Wycombe Wanderers	2-0
Willington vs Swindon Victoria	1-2

Semi-Finals

Bishop Auckland vs Loftus Albion	2-1
(at South Bank)	
Swindon Victoria vs Leytonstone	3-1
(at Reading)	

Final

Bishop Auckland vs Swindon Victoria	4-2
(at Ayresome Park, Middlesbrough 16 April 1921)	

Attendance: 25,000

Bishop Auckland: North, Wilson, Garbutt, Nattrass, Atkinson, Kasher, Brown, Cook, Binks, Ward, Wemsley
Scorers: Cook, Ward 2, Binks
Swindon Victoria: Weston, Saunders, Poole, Roberts, Cooper, Summers, Rees, Blumsdon, Eggleton, Dawson, Chivers
Scorers: Roberts, Poole (penalty)
Referee: T.S. Sephton (Derby)

1921-22 Amateur Cup

First Round

Barking Town vs Barnet	3-1
Bishop Auckland vs Langley Park	4-0
Botwell Mission vs Slough	1-1
Bournemouth Gasworks Athletic versus	
Royal Corps of Signals	2-1
Bromley vs Clapton	2-1
Calverley vs Marine	1-2
Cambridge Town vs Leytonstone	1-1
Cockfield vs Willington	4-1
Custon House vs Oxford City	0-0
Edmonton vs Nunhead	2-4
Esh Winning vs Crook Town	5-0
Eston United vs Stockton	1-1
Evesham Town vs Clifton Colliery	1-2
Hampstead Town vs Civil Service	2-0
Hathersage vs Grimsby Maycroft Rovers	3-1
Ilford vs London Caledonians	3-2
Kings Lynn vs Ipswich Town	3-3
Leeds Malvern vs Darlington R.A.	2-2
Luton Clarence vs Northampton Nomads	3-3
Metrogas vs Wimbledon	2-1
Percy Main Amateurs vs Stanley United	1-2
R.A.M.C. (Aldershot) vs Hastings & St. Leonards	2-2

Royal Marine Artillery vs Farnham United Breweries	1-1
St. Albans City vs Sutton United	3-2
Sneinton vs Boots Athletic	1-3
South Bank vs Loftus Albion	3-0
South Bank East End vs Lazenby Institute	2-0
Swansea Amateurs vs Cardiff Corinthians	0-1
Swindon Victoria vs Timsbury Athletic	2-0
Tufnell Park vs Windsor & Eton	1-3
Woolwich vs Dulwich Hamlet	0-2
Wycombe Wanderers vs Enfield	7-2

First Round Replays

Darlington R.A. vs Leeds Malvern	2-3
Farnham United Breweries vs Royal Marine Artillery	0-2
Hastings & St. Leonards vs R.A.M.C. (Aldershot)	0-2
Ipswich Town vs Kings Lynn	3-0
Leytonstone vs Cambridge Town	3-1
Northampton Nomads vs Luton Clarence	4-1
Oxford City vs Custom House	2-0
Slough vs Botwell Mission	1-4
Stockton vs Eston United	2-0

Second Round

Barking Town vs Ipswich Town	5-0
Boots Athletic vs Hathersage	5-1
Bromley vs Wycombe Wanderers	6-0
Botwell Mission vs Windsor & Eton	0-3
Cardiff Corinthians vs Hampstead Town	5-0
Clifton Colliery vs Stanley United	2-1
(at Bishop Auckland)	
Cockfield vs South Bank	1-5
Dulwich Hamlet vs Leytonstone	4-3
Esh Winning vs Bishop Auckland	0-2
Ilford vs R.A.M.C. (Aldershot)	3-1
Leeds Malvern vs South Bank East End	4-3
(at Elland Road)	
Metrogas vs Bournemouth Gasworks Athletic	2-0
Northampton Nomads vs Nunhead	5-0
St. Albans City vs Oxford City	3-2
Stockton vs Marine	4-0
Swindon Victoria vs Royal Marine Artillery	1-2

Third Round

Barking Town vs Bromley	2-1
Bishop Auckland vs Cardiff Corinthians	2-1
Boots Athletic vs Stockton	0-1
Ilford vs Windsor & Eton	0-1
Metrogas vs Clifton Colliery	2-1
Northampton Nomads vs South Bank	3-4
Royal Marine Artillery vs Leeds Malvern	1-1
St. Albans City vs Dulwich Hamlet	2-2

Third Round Replays

Dulwich Hamlet vs St. Albans City	3-1
Leeds Malvern vs Royal Marine Artillery	1-2

Fourth Round

Barking Town vs Stockton	5-2
Dulwich Hamlet vs Windsor & Eton	4-0
Royal Marine Artillery vs Bishop Auckland	0-1
South Bank vs Metrogas	2-0

Semi-Finals

Dulwich Hamlet vs Bishop Auckland	1-1
(at Fulham)	
South Bank vs Barking Town	4-1
(at Darlington)	

Semi-Final Replay

Bishop Auckland vs Dulwich Hamlet	3-0
(at Darlington)	

Final

South Bank vs Bishop Auckland	2-5
(at Ayresome Park, Middlesbrough 1 April 1922)	

Attendance: 20,000

Bishop Auckland: Potts, Wilson, Taylor, Nattrass, Atkinson, Maddison, Burrows, Cook, Binks, Mullen, Goldsborough
Scorers: Cook, Mullen, Binks 2, Nattrass
South Bank: Burns, Thomspson, Thomas, Lloyd, Brighton, Tubb, Spencer, Peacock, Towse, Hepworth, Robinson
Scorer: Peacock 2
Referee: A. Warner (Notts)

1922-23 Amateur Cup

First Round

Appleby Bridge vs Marine	5-1
Barking Town vs Chesham Town	4-2
Barnet vs Nunhead	1-2
Bournemouth Gasworks Athletic versus Hastings & St. Leonards	1-0
Civil Service vs Cowley	0-0
Clifton Colliery vs Spalding United	0-0
Crook Town vs Langley Park	5-2
Custom House vs Ilford	0-2
Dulwich Hamlet vs Leavesden Mental Hospital	0-2
Eastbourne vs Bournemouth Tramways	0-0
Eston United vs Leeds Malvern	4-1
Evesham Town vs Norfolk Amateurs	2-1
Grays Athletic vs Hampstead Town	3-1

Heaton Stannington vs Stockton	0-3
H.M.S. Excellent vs R.A.M.C. (Aldershot)	1-2
Hoylake Trinity vs Calverley	3-1
Ipswich Town vs Clapton	0-1
London Caledonians vs Slough	10-2
Loftus Albion vs West Auckland Town	1-4
Oxford City vs Gorleston	5-2
Players Athletic vs Boots Athletic	1-1
St. Albans City vs R.A.F. (Uxbridge)	8-0
Southall vs Windsor & Eton	4-0
South Bank vs Bishop Auckland	1-1
Summerstown vs Bromley	2-1
Tow Law vs Cockfield	1-2
Tufnell Park vs Leytonstone	0-5
Willington vs Esh Winning	0-1
Wimbledon vs Northampton Nomads	0-2
Woking vs Erith & Belvedere	1-1*
Wycombe Wanderers vs Kings Lynn	6-4
Swindon Victoria received a bye	
* match abandoned	

First Round Replays

Bishop Auckland vs South Bank	4-0
Bournemouth Tramways vs Eastbourne	0-1
Boots Athletic vs Players Athletic	2-1
Cowley vs Civil Service	0-1
Erith & Belvedere vs Woking	1-1
Spalding United vs Clifton Colliery	0-2

First Round Second Replay

Erith & Belvedere vs Woking
(at Erith)	6-1

Second Round

Barking Town vs Civil Service	2-1
Boots Athletic vs Crook Town	0-1
Bournemouth Gasworks Athletic vs Clapton	0-1
Clifton Colliery vs Cockfield	0-2
Erith & Belvedere vs Swindon Victoria	1-0
Esh Winning vs Apperley Bridge	2-0
Eston United vs Hoylake Trinity	6-0
Evesham Town vs West Auckland Town	5-1
Ilford vs Oxford City	1-1
Leavesden Mental Hospital vs Grays Athletic	1-0
Northampton Nomads vs Leytonstone	5-1
Nunhead vs Southall	0-2
R.A.M.C. (Aldershot) vs London Caledonians	1-1
Stockton vs Bishop Auckland	2-0
Summerstown vs Eastbourne	2-1
Wycombe Wanderers vs St. Albans City	1-2

Second Round Replays

London Caledonians vs R.A.M.C. (Aldershot)	2-0

Oxford City vs Ilford	0-1

Third Round

Erith & Belvedere vs Clapton	4-3
Esh Winning vs Cockfield	0-1
Eston United vs Stockton	2-1
Evesham Town vs Crook Town	1-0
Northampton Nomads vs
Leavesden Mental Hospital	2-1
St. Albans City vs Barking Town	4-1
Southall vs Ilford	1-1
Summerstown vs London Caledonians	0-2

Third Round Replay

Ilford vs Southall	7-2

Fourth Round

Cockfield vs Erith & Belvedere	4-0
Evesham Town vs Eston United	2-1
Ilford vs London Caledonians	0-1
Northampton Nomads vs St. Albans City	0-1

Semi-Finals

Cockfield vs Evesham Town
(at Bishop Auckland)	2-4
St. Albans City vs London Caledonians
(at Luton)	0-2

Final

London Caledonians vs Evesham Town
(at Crystal Palace 21 April 1923)	2-1

Attendance: 14,132

London Caledonians: Dawson, B. Gates, E. Gates, Blyth, Barr, Finn, McGubbin, Noble, Sloan, May, Hamilton
Scorers: May, McGubbin
Evesham Town: R. Jones, Stokes, Bridges, Gould, Ratcliff, Pennell, Hampton, Busby, Meaking, S. Jones, Osborne
Scorer: S. Jones
Referee: A.H. Kingscott (Derby)

1923-24 Amateur Cup

First Round

Attercliffe United vs Northern Nomads	2-1
Aylesbury United vs Leavesden Mental Hospital	2-2†
Barnet vs Chesham United	4-1
Bishop Auckland vs Willington	1-0
Boots Athletic vs Evesham Town	2-1
Botwell Mission vs Royal Naval Depot	3-1

Bristol St. George vs Bournemouth Gasworks Athletic	1-0
Bromley vs Nunhead	1-1
Chilton Colliery vs Guisborough Belmont Athletic	5-0
Clapton vs Ipswich Town	4-0
Clifton Colliery vs Players Athletic	0-2
Cockfield vs South Bank	1-0
Custom House vs Barking Town	1-2
Dulwich Hamlet vs Farnham United Breweries	4-1
Erith & Belvedere vs Slough	5-3
Esh Winning vs St. Peter's Albion	3-1
Eston United vs Langley Park	3-1
Grays Athletic vs Ilford	0-2
Leytonstone vs Gorleston	1-0
London Caledonians vs Civil Service	1-0
Marine vs Rawdon (Leeds)	2-1
Northampton Nomads vs Oxford City	4-2
R.A.F. (Cranwell) vs Badsey Rangers	2-1
Redhill vs Summerstown	1-1†
St. Albans City vs Wycombe Wanderers	1-1
Southall vs Casuals	3-1
Staines Lagonda vs Wimbledon	1-0
Stockton vs Apperley Bridge	1-1
Tow Law Town vs Crook Town	5-3
Tufnell Park vs R.M.L.I. (Chatham)	0-2
Wells City vs Bournemouth	1-3
Worthing vs Royal Marines (Portsmouth)	1-2
† match abandoned during extra time	

First Round Replays

Apperley Bridge vs Stockton	0-5
Leavesden Mental Hospital vs Aylesbury United	1-2
Nunhead vs Bromley	3-1
Summerstown vs Redhill	1-0
Wycombe Wanderers vs St. Albans City	2-1

Second Round

Attercliffe United vs Stockton	1-0
Aylesbury United vs Northampton Nomads	1-1†
Barking Town vs London Caledonians	1-2
Boots Athletic vs Players Athletic	2-1
Botwell Mission vs Bristol St. George	6-1
Bournemouth vs Barnet	3-1
Chilton Colliery vs Tow Law Town	3-0
Clapton vs Southall	3-0
Esh Winning vs R.A.F. (Cranwell)	1-1
Eston United vs Bishop Auckland	0-1
Leytonstone vs Dulwich Hamlet	1-4
Marine vs Cockfield	3-0
Nunhead vs Royal Marines (Portsmouth)	0-0*, 1-1
R.M.L.I. (Chatham) vs Erith & Belvedere	2-2
Summerstown vs Staines Lagonda	1-1†
Wycombe Wanderers vs Ilford	1-0
* match abandoned	
† abandoned during extra time	

Second Round Replays

Erith & Belvedere vs R.M.L.I. (Chatham)	4-1
Northampton Nomads vs Aylesbury United	10-1
R.A.F. (Cranwell) vs Esh Winning	1-2
Royal Marines (Portsmouth) vs Nunhead	1-1
Staines Lagonda vs Summerstown	2-1

Second Round Second Replay

Nunhead vs Royal Marines (Portsmouth) (at Portsmouth)	1-2

Third Round

Attercliffe United vs Dulwich Hamlet	1-2
Boots Athletic vs Northampton Nomads	3-5
Bournemouth vs Botwell Mission	0-1
Chilton Colliery vs Bishop Auckland	2-0
Clapton vs Royal Marines (Portsmouth)	6-1
Erith & Belvedere vs Esh Winning	1-0
London Caledonians vs Marine	5-0
Staines Lagonda vs Wycombe Wanderers	1-2

Fourth Round

Botwell Mission vs Erith & Belvedere	0-3
Dulwich Hamlet vs Chilton Colliery	1-1
Northampton Nomads vs Clapton	2-4
Wycombe Wanderers vs London Caledonians	0-3

Fourth Round Replay

Chilton Colliery vs Dulwich Hamlet	3-0

Semi-Finals

Chilton Colliery vs Clapton (at Darlington)	0-3
Erith & Belvedere vs London Caledonians (at Crystal Palace)	1-1

Semi-Final Replay

Erith & Belvedere vs London Caledonians (at Crystal Palace)	0-0

Semi-Final Second Replay

London Caledonians vs Erith & Belvedere (at Stamford Bridge)	1-3

Final

Erith & Belvedere vs Clapton   0-3
(at The Den, Millwall 5 April 1924)

Attendance: 32,000

Clapton: Moore, Penstone, Blake, Williams, Bryant,
Cable, Riley, Earle, Gibbins, Pooter, Barnard
Scorers: Potter 2, Barnard
Erith & Belvedere: C. Evans, R. Evans, Wilson, Marks,
Duffy, Swayne, Gooch, McKee, Yates, Hillier, Beckford
Referee: F. Todman (Surrey)

1924-25 Amateur Cup

First Round

Aldershot Traction Company vs Wycombe Wanderers	3-1
Bishop Auckland vs South Bank	2-1
Botwell Mission vs Barnet	0-2
Bournemouth vs Royal Marines (Portsmouth)	3-5
Bournemouth Gasworks Athletic versus	
Hastings & St. Leonards	1-1
Bromley vs St. Albans City	0-5
Cambridge Town vs Northampton Nomads	2-0
Chilton Colliery vs Stockton Shamrock	2-1
Civil Service vs Tufnell Park	0-2
Clapton vs London Caledonians	2-0
Clevedon vs Welton Rovers	2-1
Crook Town vs Stockton	1-1
Dulwich Hamlet vs Enfield	1-1
Eastbourne vs Portsea Island Gas Company	1-1
Grays Athletic vs Southall	0-4
Hallam vs Whitehall Printeries	0-0
Hampstead Town vs Casuals	2-0
Hull Young People's Institute vs Attercliffe United	0-2
Humber (Coventry) vs Evesham Town	2-5
Ilford vs Chesham Town	1-0
Kingstonian vs Leyton	0-1
Langley Park vs Cockfield	2-1
Lenton vs Boots Athletic	0-2
Leytonstone vs Oxford City	1-2
Loftus Albion vs Ferryhill Athletic	2-3
Marine vs Northern Nomads	0-3
Mitcham Wanderers vs Erith & Belvedere	3-1
Nunhead vs Summerstown	3-1
Players Athletic vs R.A.F. (Cranwell)	5-1
Staines Lagonda vs Leighton United	4-2
Tow Law Town vs Eston United	7-1
Wimbledon vs Bostall Heath	0-3

First Round Replays

Enfield vs Dulwich Hamlet	0-4
Hastings & St. Leonards versus	
Bournemouth Gasworks Athletic	4-0

Portsea Island Gas Company vs Eastbourne	1-0
Stockton vs Crook Town	4-0
Whitehall Printeries vs Hallam	0-1
(at Elland Road)	

Second Round

Barnet vs Staines Lagonda	2-0
Bishop Auckland vs Tow Law Town	3-2
Boots Athletic vs Players Athletic	3-6
Cambridge Town vs Clevedon	3-1
Chilton Colliery vs Stockton	2-1
Clapton vs Mitcham Wanderers	3-1
Dulwich Hamlet vs Aldershot Traction Company	3-1
Hallam vs Attercliffe United	0-0
Hampstead Town vs Bostall Heath	1-3
Hastings & St. Leonards vs St. Albans City	1-7
Ilford vs Southall	0-1
Langley Park vs Ferryhill Athletic	3-2
Northern Nomads vs Evesham Town	3-1
Nunhead vs Royal Marines (Portsmouth)	2-0
Oxford City vs Leyton	4-2
Tufnell Park vs Portsea Island Gas Company	8-0

Second Round Replay

Attercliffe United vs Hallam	1-3

Third Round

Bostall Heath vs St. Albans City	0-1
Cambridge Town vs Clapton	1-3
Chilton Colliery vs Langley Park	3-0
Hallam vs Bishop Auckland	2-1
Nunhead vs Dulwich Hamlet	1-1*
* abandoned during extra time	
Oxford City vs Barnet	2-5
Players Athletic vs Northern Nomads	2-3
Tufnell Park vs Southall	1-4

Third Round Replay

Dulwich Hamlet vs Nunhead	2-1

Fourth Round

Barnet vs St. Albans City	1-2
Chilton Colliery vs Northern Nomads	0-2
Clapton vs Hallam	1-0
Southall vs Dulwich Hamlet	1-0

Semi-Finals

Clapton vs Northern Nomads	2-1
(at Ilford)	
St. Albans City vs Southall	1-1
(at Watford)	

Semi-Final Replay

Southall vs St. Albans City   1-0
(at Brentford)

Final

Clapton vs Southall   2-1
(at The Den, Millwall 18 April 1925)

Attendance: 25,000

Clapton: Moore, Penstone, Blake, Williams, Bryant, Cable, Ryley, Potter, Gibbins, Miller, Barnard
Scorer: Gibbins 2
Southall: Holding, Buttery, Gower, Johnson, Harvey, Wenham, Jance, Jackson, Clark, Corban, Hawkins, Howell
Scorer: Hawkins
Referee: F.C. Winton (Sussex)

1925-26 Amateur Cup

First Round

Barking Town vs Leyton	0-4
Basford United vs Attercliffe United	5-2
Barnet vs Hampstead Town	3-5
1st Battalion Middlesex Regiment versus London Caledonians	1-4
Bishop Auckland vs Stockton	2-2
Bostall Heath vs Nunhead	1-5
Botwell Mission vs Kingstonian	1-2
Bournemouth vs Portland United	1-2
Cambridge Town vs Great Yarmouth Town	3-2
Casuals vs Oxford City	6-4*
* a replay was ordered after a protest	
Chesham United vs Redhill	1-2
Cheshunt vs H.M.S. Excellent	3-2
Chilton Colliery Recreation vs Cockfield	2-0
Civil Service vs Southall	2-2
Erith & Belvedere vs Eastbourne	5-1
Ferryhill Atheltic vs Langley Park	4-1
G.E.R. (Romford) vs Northampton Nomads	3-1
Hallam vs Players Athletic	9-4
Hanwell Town vs Uxbridge Town	1-3
Humber Recreation vs Whitehall Printeries	2-4
Kingswood vs Welton Rovers	1-2
Leytonstone vs Leagrave & District	1-1
Northern Nomads vs Furness Withy	2-0
Norton Woodseats vs Boots Athletic	3-1
Percy Main Amateurs vs Crook Town	1-4
R.A.F. (Cranwell) vs Evesham Town	0-2
St. Albans City vs Clapton	3-1
Scarborough vs South Bank	7-2
Tow Law Town vs Stockton Shamrock	2-2
Tufnell Park vs Ilford	1-6
West Norwood vs Dulwich Hamlet	0-5

Wycombe Wanderers vs Hove	10-2

First Round Replays

Leagrave & District vs Leytonstone	1-6
Oxford City vs Casuals	1-0
Southall vs Civil Service	4-1
Stockton vs Bishop Auckland	5-1
Stockton Shamrock vs Tow Law Town	2-3

Second Round

Crook Town vs Chilton Colliery Recreation	3-1
Ferryhill Athletic vs Tow Law Town	2-1
G.E.R. (Romford) vs London Caledonians	1-1
Hallam vs Basford United	5-1
Hampstead Town vs Wycombe Wanderers	1-0
Kingstonian vs Redhill	1-4
Leytonstone vs Cambridge Town	3-0
Northern Nomads vs Whitehall Printeries	5-2
Norton Woodseats vs Evesham Town	3-1
Nunhead vs Erith & Belvedere	3-2
Oxford City vs Dulwich Hamlet	5-1
Portland United vs Leyton	1-1
St. Albans City vs Cheshunt	3-1
Scarborough vs Stockton	1-3
Southall vs Welton Rovers	3-1
Uxbridge Town vs Ilford	3-3

Second Round Replays

Ilford vs Uxbridge Town	10-2
Leyton vs Portland United	4-1
London Caledonians vs G.E.R. (Romford)	3-1

Third Round

Ferryhill Athletic vs Hampstead Town	4-0
Northern Nomads vs Hallam	5-1
Norton Woodseats vs Crook Town	1-1
Nunhead vs Leytonstone	5-1
Oxford City vs Leyton	2-3
Redhill vs Ilford	4-1
Southall vs St. Albans City	1-1
Stockton vs London Caledonians	2-1

Third Round Replays

Crook Town vs Norton Woodseats	4-2
St. Albans City vs Southall	3-2

Fourth Round

Crook Town vs Northern Nomads	1-3
Redhill vs Leyton	3-2
St. Albans City vs Ferryhill Athletic	4-1
Stockton vs Nunhead	2-1

Semi-Finals

Redhill vs Northern Nomads	1-7
(at Highbury)	
Stockton vs St. Albans City	2-1
(at Middlesbrough)	

Final

Northern Nomads vs Stockton	7-1
(at Roker Park, Sunderland 17 April 1926)	

Attendance: 13,300

Northern Nomads: Menham, Blair, Abbott, Jones, Fairweather, Waker, Loxham, Robertston, Beswick, Randle, Fairclough
Scorers: Beswick 3, Randall 3, Robertson
Stockton: Murray, Longstaff, Shanks, Lowther, Scaife, Pritchard, Evans, Clare, Thompson, Pass, McGiffen
Scorer: Thompson
Referee: A. Scholey (Sheffield & Hallamshire)

1926-27 Amateur Cup

First Round

Barking Town vs Kingstonian	6-1
Barnet vs Eastbourne Comrades	3-0
Boots Athletic vs Birmingham Tramways	1-2
Botwell Mission vs Chesham United	4-3
Bournville vs 6th Durham Light Infantry	1-2
Bromley vs Cray Wanderers	3-1
Chilton Colliery vs Bishop Auckland	1-1
Crook Town vs Players Athletic	3-1
Ferryhill Athletic vs Sutton Junction	6-2
Finchley vs Leyton	0-3
G.E.R. (Romford) vs Portland United	1-3
Great Yarmouth Town vs Nunhead	0-1
Guiseley vs Loftus Albion	4-2
Hallam vs Esh Winning	1-1
Hampstead Town vs Casuals	3-3
H.M.S. Excellent vs Southall	2-3
Leytonstone vs Dulwich Hamlet	1-3
London Caledonians vs Cambridge Town	4-1
Northern Nomads vs Percy Main Amateurs	4-0
Oxford City vs Blandford United	6-0
Redhill vs Northampton Nomads	4-1
Rotherham Amateurs vs Stockton Malle	0-0
South Bank vs Norton Woodseats	1-0
Stockton vs Hull Old Boys	7-0
Tufnell Park vs Clapton	4-2
Uxbridge Town vs Kingswood (Bristol)	0-1
Wealdstone vs Maidenhead United	1-2
Welton Rovers vs Eastbourne	4-0
Willington vs Marine (Liverpool)	5-3
Wimbledon vs Ilford	1-1

Woking vs St. Albans City	1-4
Wycombe Wanderers vs Walthamstow Avenue	3-2

First Round Replays

Bishop Auckland vs Chilton Colliery	0-0
Casuals vs Hampstead Town	3-2
Esh Winning vs Hallam	2-1
Ilford vs Wimbledon	4-0
Stockton Malle vs Rotherham Amateurs	2-0

First Round Second Replay

Chilton Colliery vs Bishop Auckland	1-0
(at Chilton)	

Second Round

Crook Town vs Willington	3-0
Dulwich Hamlet vs Botwell Mission	6-1
Esh Winning vs Northern Nomads	1-3
Guiseley vs Chilton Colliery	1-6
Leyton vs Oxford City	8-0
Maidenhead United vs Bromley	3-2
Nunhead vs Tufnell Park	2-2
Portland United vs Casuals	2-3
Redhill vs Barking	1-2
St. Albans City vs Barnet	6-1
Southall vs Ilford	3-2
South Bank vs 6th Durham Light Infantry	1-1
Stockton vs Birmingham Tramways	4-0
Stockton Malle vs Ferryhill Athletic	2-7
Welton Rovers vs Kingswood (Bristol)	2-1
Wycombe Wanderers vs London Caledonians	3-2

Second Round Replays

6th Durham Light Infantry vs South Bank	1-6
(at Bishop Auckland)	
Tufnell Park vs Nunhead	0-3

Third Round

Barking Town vs Maidenhead United	3-1
Leyton vs Northern Nomads	2-1
Nunhead vs Ferryhill Athletic	6-2
St. Albans City vs Crook Town	0-2
Southall vs Casuals	4-2
Stockton vs Dulwich Hamlet	1-1
Welton Rovers vs South Bank	3-3
Wycombe Wanderers vs Chilton Colliery	3-1

Third Round Replays

Dulwich Hamlet vs Stockton	7-2
South Bank vs Welton Rovers	6-2

Fourth Round

Barking Town vs Wycombe Wanderers	3-2
Nunhead vs Leyton	1-2
Southall vs Crook Town	4-0
South Bank vs Dulwich Hamlet	2-1

Semi-Finals

Southall vs Leyton	2-2
(at Chelsea)	
South Bank vs Barking Town	1-2
(at Auckland)	

Semi-Final Replay

Leyton vs Southall	2-1
(at Fulham)	

Final

Barking Town vs Leyton	1-3
(at The Den, Millwall 9 April 1927)	

Attendance: 12,864

Leyton: Grainger, Preston, Terris, Graves, Cable, Goldsmith, Salmons, Hall, Bowyer, Smith, T. Hawkins
Scorers: Cable 2, Salmons
Barking Town: McCracken, Carmen, Norrington, Kemp, Jango, Young, Evans, J. Hawkins, Scarborough, Guyton, Lucas
Scorer: Hawkins
Referee: H.N. Mee (Notts)

1927-28 Amateur Cup

First Round

Barking Town vs Northampton Nomads	9-1
Barnet vs Chesham United	4-2
Bournville Athletic vs Hallam	2-6
Cambridge Town vs R.A.S.C. (Aldershot)	3-1
Chilton Colliery vs Boots Athletic	6-0
Chippenham Town vs Dulwich Hamlet	2-3
Civil Service vs Ilford	1-5
Clapton vs Sutton United	1-2
Crook Town vs Bishop Auckland	2-1
Enfield vs London Caledonians	1-5
Ferryhill Athletic vs Esh Winning	0-5
Great Yarmouth Town vs St. Albans City	2-2
Hampstead Town vs Royal Naval Depot	1-2
Hanham Athletic vs Portland United	1-3
Kingstonian vs Redhill	3-5
Leyton vs Bromley	4-4
Maidenhead United vs Leytonstone	2-0*, 1-3
* match abandoned	
Marine (Liverpool) vs Northern Nomads	2-0

Norton Woodseats vs Cockfield	1-1
Nunhead vs 5th Battalion Royal Tank Corps	5-3
Player's Athletic vs Filey Town	7-0
Rawmarsh Welfare vs Stockton	1-1
R.N. (Portsmouth) vs Grays Athletic	3-4
Stockton Shamrocks vs Sutton Junction	2-1
Tow Law Town vs South Bank	4-2
Tufnell Park vs Eastbourne	4-3
Welton Rovers vs Southall	3-4
Whitehall Printeries vs Willington	2-3
Whitby United vs Birmingham Tramways	1-1
Wimbledon vs Oxford City	3-1
Woking vs Casuals	2-2
Wycombe Wanderers vs Southwick	4-2

First Round Replays

Birmingham Tramways vs Whitby United	2-6
Bromley vs Leyton	1-4
Casuals vs Woking	1-5
Cockfield vs Norton Woodseats	1-0
St. Albans City vs Great Yarmouth Town	6-0
Stockton vs Rawmarsh Welfare	7-0

Second Round

Barnet vs Dulwich Hamlet	2-1
Bishop Auckland vs Tow Law Town	2-0
Cambridge Town vs Wycombe Wanderers	1-1
Cockfield vs Stockton Shamrock	3-0
Hallam vs Marine (Liverpool)	2-1
Leyton vs Redhill	5-1
Nunhead vs Sutton United	3-2
Player's Athletic vs Whitby United	2-1
Portland United vs Barking Town	1-3
St. Albans City vs Ilford	3-2
Southall vs Grays Athletic	1-0
Stockton vs Chilton Colliery	3-1
Tufnell Park vs Leytonstone	1-3
Willington vs Esh Winning	6-0
Wimbledon vs Royal Naval Depot	4-2
Woking vs London Caledonians	0-1

Second Round Replay

Wycombe Wanderers vs Cambridge Town	3-0

Third Round

Barking Town vs London Caledonians	0-0
Barnet vs Hallam	3-1
Bishop Auckland vs Southall	2-1
Cambridge Town vs Stockton	2-1
Nunhead vs Leyton	1-2
St. Albans City vs Cockfield	0-1
Willington vs Player's Athletic	5-1
Wimbledon vs Leytonstone	0-3

Third Round Replay

London Caledonians vs Barking Town	0-1

Fourth Round

Barking Town vs Cambridge Town	2-3
Bishop Auckland vs Cockfield	0-0
Leyton vs Leytonstone	3-0
Willington vs Barnet	2-1

Fourth Round Replay

Cockfield vs Bishop Auckland	2-1

Semi-Finals

Cockfield vs Willington	2-2
(at Darlington)	
Leyton vs Cambridge Town	5-2
(at Fulham)	

Semi-Final Replay

Willington vs Cockfield	1-2
(at Bishop Auckland)	

Final

Cockfield vs Leyton	2-3
(at Ayresome Park, Middlesbrough 14 April 1928)	

Attendance: 12,200

Leyton: Burr, Preston, Goldsmith, Graves, Cable, Margetts, McKinley, Hall, Avey, Smith, Hawkins
Scorers: McKinley, Smith, Cable
Cockfield: Wedge, Dixon, Coates, Barker, Harrison, Oldfield, Longstaffe, Pearson, Rutter, Thompson, Kirby
Scorer: Rutter 2
Referee: R. Brown (Northumberland)

1928-29 Amateur Cup

First Round

Aldershot Traction Company vs Portland United	2-1
Barking Town vs Woking	6-1
Birmingham Tramways vs Player's Athletic	1-1
Bournemouth Gasworks Athletic vs Tufnell Park	3-0
Bromley vs Wimbledon	2-1
Cambridge Town vs Oxford City	2-2
Chesham United vs St. Albans City	1-0
Clapton vs Nunhead	2-0
Colchester Town vs Barnet	1-7
Eastbourne vs Dulwich Hamlet	1-7
Evenwood Town vs Pilkington Recreation	4-1*
* Evenwood Town were disqualified	
Filey vs West Hartlepool Perseverance	3-5

Gorleston vs Southall	1-1
Hanham Athletic vs Leytonstone	1-1
Kingstonian vs Leyton	0-1
London Caledonians vs Hastings & St. Leonards	1-0
Maidenhead United vs Hampstead Town	2-4
Marine vs Moor Green	5-0
Norton Woodseats vs Whitehall Printeries	2-3
Percy Main Amateurs vs Boots Athletic	7-0
Royal Naval Depot (Chatham) vs Bexleyheath	4-1
Sneinton vs Bournville Athletic	2-0
South Bank vs Northern Nomads	6-6
Southwick vs Casuals	2-2
Stockton vs Hull Old Boys	8-0
Sutton United vs H.M.S. Excellent	3-0
Tow Law Town vs Blundellsands	6-1
Wealdstone vs Ilford	3-3
Welton Rovers vs Redhill	3-0
Whitby United vs Hallam	1-1
Wycombe Wanderers vs Aylesbury United	3-1
Yorkshire Amateurs vs Stockton Shamrock	4-0

First Round Replays

Casuals vs Southwick	2-3
Hallam vs Whitby United	4-3
Ilford vs Wealdstone	8-0
Leytonstone vs Hanham Athletic	6-3
Northern Nomads vs South Bank	2-2
Oxford City vs Cambridge Town	4-2
Players Athletic vs Birmingham Tramways	5-0
Southall vs Gorleston	1-1

First Round Second Replays

Gorleston vs Southall	2-2
(at Ipswich)	
South Bank vs Northern Nomads	0-3
(at Scarborough)	

First Round Third Replay

Gorleston vs Southall	2-1
(at Ipswich)	

Second Round

Aldershot Traction Company vs Barking Town	4-1
Barnet vs Welton Rovers	2-3
Clapton vs R.N. Depot (Chatham)	5-4
Dulwich Hamlet vs Bromley	4-2
Gorleston vs Ilford	0-3
Hallam vs Sneinton	6-4
London Caledonians vs Leyton	0-1
Northern Nomads vs Percy Main Amateurs	5-0
Oxford City vs Leytonstone	0-3
Southwick vs Chesham United	2-1
Stockton vs West Hartlepool Perseverance	4-1

Sutton United vs Hampstead Town	4-3
Tow Law Town vs Players Athletic	4-1
Whitehall Printeries vs Marine	4-1
Wycombe Wanderers versus	
Bournemouth Gasworks Athletic	5-2
Yorkshire Amateurs vs Pilkington Recreation	3-0

Third Round

Dulwich Hamlet vs Wycombe Wanderers	7-1
Hallam vs Welton Rovers	0-3
Leyton vs Yorkshire Amateurs	4-0
Northern Nomads vs Ilford	2-4
Southwick vs Clapton	1-2
Stockton vs Tow Law Town	3-1
Sutton United vs Leytonstone	6-3
Whitehall Printeries vs Aldershot Traction Company	3-5

Fourth Round

Clapton vs Welton Rovers	5-1
Dulwich Hamlet vs Aldershot Traction Company	7-0
Ilford vs Stockton	4-2
Leyton vs Sutton United	0-1

Semi-Finals

Dulwich Hamlet vs Ilford	1-4
(at Stamford Bridge)	
Leyton vs Clapton	2-1
(at Ilford)	

Final

Ilford vs Leyton	3-1
(at Highbury Stadium, London 20 April 1929)	

Attendance: 35,000

Ilford: Norman, Banks, Wade, Gilderson, Craymer, Barron, Potter, Welsh, Dellow, Drane, Peploe
Scorers: Drane, Peploe, Potter
Leyton: Jones, Preston, Goldsmith, Graves, Wright, Margetts, Collins, Hall, Ives, Smith, Hawkins
Scorer: Smith
Referee: C.E. Lines (Birmingham)

1929-30 Amateur Cup

First Round

Barking Town vs Maidenhead United	5-1
Bournemouth Gasworks Athletic versus	
Wycombe Wanderers	2-1
Chesham United vs Kings Lynn	3-2
Clapton vs Barnet	0-4
Dulwich Hamlet vs Casuals	4-0
Enfield vs St. Albans City	2-0

Esh Winning vs Birmingham Tramways	4-0
Gorleston vs Portland United	4-0
Grays Athletic vs Lowestoft Town	8-1
Hampstead Town vs Woking	3-2
Ilford vs Eastbourne	13-1
Kingstonian vs Hounslow	1-0
Leyton vs Colefield Athletic	7-0
Leytonstone vs London Caledonians	0-6
Malvern Holy Trinity vs Hallam	3-3
Metropolitan Police vs Bromley	2-1
Nunhead vs Berkhamsted Town	10-0
Percy Main Amateurs vs Cleethorpes Town	2-2
Pilkington Recreation vs Marine	2-2
Players Athletic vs Evenwood Town	2-2
Rawmarsh Welfare vs Egglescliffe	2-1
Sneinton vs Horsforth	2-3
Southall vs H.M.S. Excellent	0-0
South Bank vs Yorkshire Amateurs	0-2
Southwick vs Cambridge Town	0-2
Stanley United vs Norton Woodseats	1-0
Stockton vs Whitehall Printeries	4-1
Tow Law Town vs R.A.F. (Grantham)	4-2
Tufnell Park vs R.N. Depot (Chatham)	3-1
Welton Rovers vs Kingswood	4-1
Whitby United vs Northern Nomads	2-4
Wimbledon vs Aldershot Traction Company	4-3

First Round Replays

Cleethorpes Town vs Percy Main Amateurs	3-4
Evenwood Town vs Players Athletic	5-0
Hallam vs Malvern Holy Trinity	6-4
H.M.S. Excellent vs Southall	3-2*
* abandoned during extra time	
Marine vs Pilkington Recreation	7-1

First Round Second Replay

H.M.S. Excellent vs Southall	3-1
(at Redhill)	

Second Round

Barnet vs H.M.S. Excellent	2-1
Bournemouth Gasworks Athletic vs Welton Rovers	4-0
Cambridge Town vs Wimbledon	0-2
Dulwich Hamlet vs Tufnell Park	4-3
Enfield vs Metropolitan Police	0-2
Esh Winning vs Stockton	3-3
Evenwood Town vs Horsforth	3-1
Gorleston vs Leyton	0-1
Hampstead Town vs Barking Town	1-4
Kingstonian vs Grays Athletic	4-1
London Caledonians vs Ilford	1-3
Northern Nomads vs Hallam	3-1
Nunhead vs Chesham United	1-3
Percy Main Amateurs vs Rawmarsh Welfare	3-0

Tow Law Town vs Marine	2-1
Yorkshire Amateurs vs Stanley United	3-0

Second Round Replay

Stockton vs Esh Winning	4-0

Third Round

Bournemouth Gasworks Athletic vs Barnet	3-1
Dulwich Hamlet v Chesham United	2-0
Ilford vs Evenwood Town	3-0
Kingstonian vs Leyton	0-1
Percy Main Amateurs vs Yorkshire Amateurs	1-1
Stockton vs Barking Town	4-1
Tow Law Town vs Northern Nomads	0-3
Wimbledon vs Metropolitan Police	2-1

Third Round Replay

Yorkshire Amateurs vs Percy Main Amateurs	0-1

Fourth Round

Bournemouth Gasworks Athletic versus Percy Main Amateurs	2-0
Ilford vs Dulwich Hamlet	2-1
Leyton vs Wimbledon	0-1
Northern Nomads vs Stockton	1-0

Semi-Finals

Bournemouth Gasworks Athletic vs Wimbledon (at Portsmouth)	2-0
Ilford vs Northern Nomads (at Leyton)	0-0

Semi-Final Replay

Ilford vs Northern Nomads (at Dulwich Hamlet)	4-2

Final

Ilford vs Bournemouth Gasworks Athletic (at Upton Park, London 12 April 1930)	5-1

Attendance: 21,800

Ilford: Watson, Triesman, Winterburn, Shappard, Craymer, Webb, Potter, Welsh, Dellow, Drane, Peploe
Scorers: Dellow, Peploe 2, Welsh, Potter
Bournemouth Gasworks Athletic: Joyce, Saunders, Cobb, Turner, Phillips, Gillingham, Smith, Pettey, Lavell, Cornbeer, Tapper
Scorer: Pettey*
* some reports attribute the Bournemouth goal to Cornbeer
Referee: L.E. Gibbs (Berks and Bucks)

1930-31 Amateur Cup

First Round

Barking Town vs Bromley	5-1
Barnet vs Bournemouth Gasworks Athletic	9-3
Birmingham Gas Officials vs South Salford Amateurs	2-1
Bishop Auckland vs Evenwood Town	1-1*
Clapton vs H.M.S. Excellent	1-1
Egham vs Romford	0-3
Epsom Town vs Ilford	2-5
Hampstead Town vs Welton Rovers	2-6
Hitchin Town vs Leyton	0-3
Humber United vs Rawmarsh Welfare	1-1
Kingstonian vs Enfield	3-1
London Caledonians vs Wycombe Wanderers	1-4
Lowestoft Town vs St. Phillip's Athletic	1-0
Manningham Mills vs Percy Main Amateurs	2-1
Marine vs Whitby United	7-2
Newcastle West End Amateurs versus Chilton Colliery Recreation	2-3
Northern Nomads vs Yorkshire Amateurs	3-2
Norton Woodseats vs Normanby Magnesite	3-1
Nunhead vs Leavesden Mental Hospital	4-0
Players Athletic vs South Bank	1-0
Portland United vs Dulwich Hamlet	4-2
Royal Marines (Chatham) vs Casuals	3-4
Ryde Sports vs Maidenhead United	5-5
St. Albans City vs Wimbledon	1-5
Sneinton vs Hallam	2-0
Southwick vs Walthamstow Avenue	1-2
Stockton vs Horsforth	6-2
Trowbridge Town vs Gorleston	2-0
Whitby Albion Rangers vs Willington	4-4
Wisbech Town vs Hayes	1-6
Woking vs Cambridge Town	3-1
Worthing vs Metropolitan Police	0-3

First Round Replays

Bishop Auckland vs Evenwood Town	5-1*
H.M.S. Excellent vs Clapton	1-2
Maidenhead United vs Ryde Sports	6-1
Rawmarsh Welfare vs Humber United	1-0
Willington vs Whitby Albion Rangers	6-1
* both matches were played at Bishop Auckland	

Second Round

Barking Town vs Wimbledon	0-1
Barnet vs Clapton	1-3
Bishop Auckland vs Marine	2-1
Casuals vs Ilford	2-4
Lowestoft Town vs Welton Rovers	1-1
Maidenhead United vs Portland United	3-3
Manningham Mills vs Northern Nomads	1-2
Nunhead vs Metropolitan Police	0-2

Players Athletic vs Willington	2-3
Rawmarsh Welfare vs Chilton Colliery Recreation	3-0
Romford vs Kingstonian	5-1
Sneinton vs Birmingham Gas Officials	2-1
Stockton vs Norton Woodseats	7-2
Trowbridge Town vs Hayes	1-2
Woking vs Leyton	4-0
Wycombe Wanderers vs Walthamstow Avenue	6-1

Second Round Replays

| Portland United vs Maidenhead United | 0-0 |
| Welton Rovers vs Lowestoft Town | 2-1 |

Second Round Second Replay

| Maidenhead United vs Portland United | 2-2 |
| (at Southampton) | |

Second Round Third Replay

| Portland United vs Maidenhead United | 4-1 |
| (at Southampton) | |

Third Round

Bishop Auckland vs Ilford	6-2
Clapton vs Rawmarsh Welfare	2-1
Metropolitan Police vs Welton Rovers	3-1
Northern Nomads vs Willington	3-1
Stockton vs Sneinton	7-2
Wimbledon vs Hayes	2-3
Woking vs Portland United	2-1
Wycombe Wanderers vs Romford	6-2

Fourth Round

Bishop Auckland vs Stockton	5-3
Clapton vs Woking	0-1
Metropolitan Police vs Wycombe Wanderers	1-1
Northern Nomads vs Hayes	1-2

Fourth Round Replay

| Wycombe Wanderers vs Metropolitan Police | 2-1 |

Semi-Finals

Bishop Auckland vs Hayes	0-1
(at York)	
Wycombe Wanderers vs Woking	3-0
(at Ilford)	

Final

| Hayes vs Wycombe Wanderers | 0-1 |
| (at Highbury Stadium, London 11 April 1931) | |

Attendance: 32,000

Wycombe Wanderers: Kipping, Crump, Cox, Rance, Badrick, Greenwell, Simmons, Brown, Vernon, Braisher, Britnell
Scorer: Britnell
Hayes: Holding, Maskell, Gower, E. Caesar, Wainwright, W. Caesar, Knight, Rowe, Morgan, Welsh, Lloyd
Referee: P. Graham (Birmingham)

1931-32 Amateur Cup

First Round

Barking Town vs Wycombe Wanderers	2-3
Barnet vs Hayes	1-4
Cambridge Town vs St. Ives Town	7-4
Chesham United vs Bournemouth Gasworks Athletic	1-4
Clapton vs Welton Rovers	0-1
1st Battalion Durham Light Infantry vs Bishop Auckland	1-2
Erith & Belvedere vs Colchester Town	4-1
Excelsior Foundry vs Rawmarsh Welfare	1-6
Gorleston vs Dulwich Hamlet	1-2
Hitchin Town vs Nunhead	4-2
H.M.S. Excellent vs Portland United	0-5
Ilford vs Trowbridge Town	5-0
Ipswich Town vs Epsom Town	2-4
Keynsham vs Hampstead Town	2-7
Kingstonian vs Wealdstone	6-1
Leyton vs Southwick	3-0
London Caledonians vs Wimbledon	1-3
Maidenhead United vs Woking	4-0
Manningham Mills vs Northern Nomads	2-1
Marine vs Northampton Nomads	4-2
Moor Green vs Evenwood Town	1-3
Players Athletic vs South Salford Amateurs	4-1
R.A.F. (Grantham) vs Stanhope	2-2
St. Albans City vs Slough	2-1
Southall vs Romford	1-3
South Bank vs Sneinton	6-0
Stockton vs Norton Woodseats	4-3
Walthamstow Avenue vs Casuals	4-2
Whitby United vs Whitby Albion Rangers	3-1
Willington vs Whitehall Printeries	0-1
Worthing vs R.A.M.C. (Aldershot)	2-1
Yorkshire Amateurs vs Percy Main Amateurs	4-1

First Round Replay

| Stanhope vs R.A.F. (Grantham) | 4-3 |

Second Round

Bournemouth Gasworks Athletic vs Hayes	2-1
Dulwich Hamlet vs Cambridge Town	7-1
Erith & Belvedere vs Maidenhead United	2-4
Hampstead Town vs Portland United	0-0

Hitchin Town vs Walthamstow Avenue	2-1
Manningham Mills vs Stockton	1-2
Players Athletic vs Bishop Auckland	0-1
Romford vs Kingstonian	1-5
St. Albans City vs Wimbledon	1-4
South Bank vs Marine	1-2
Stanhope vs Rawmarsh Welfare	3-2
Welton Rovers vs Leyton	1-1
Whitehall Printeries vs Evenwood Town	3-1
Worthing vs Ilford	2-10
Wycombe Wanderers vs Epsom Town	7-2
Yorkshire Amateurs vs Whitby United	3-1

Second Round Replays

Leyton vs Welton Rovers	2-1
Portland United vs Hampstead Town	1-0

Third Round

Bishop Auckland vs Whitehall Printeries	3-1
Hitchin Town vs Wimbledon	0-2
Ilford vs Stanhope	5-1
Leyton vs Bournemouth Gasworks Athletic	3-0
Marine vs Maidenhead United	4-1
Portland United vs Kingstonian	0-3
Stockton vs Dulwich Hamlet	1-1
Yorkshire Amateurs vs Wycombe Wanderers	4-0

Third Round Replay

Dulwich Hamlet vs Stockton	3-0

Fourth Round

Dulwich Hamlet vs Ilford	2-1
Kingstonian vs Bishop Auckland	1-0
Marine vs Leyton	3-0
Wimbledon vs Yorkshire Amateurs	2-2

Fourth Round Replay

Yorkshire Amateurs vs Wimbledon	5-2

Semi-Finals

Dulwich Hamlet vs Kingstonian (at Selhurst Park)	1-0
Yorkshire Amateurs vs Marine (at Leicester)	1-2

Final

Dulwich Hamlet vs Marine	7-1

(at Upton Park, London 16 April 1932)

Attendance: 22,000

Dulwich Hamlet: Miles, Hugo, Osmond, Murray, Hamer, Aitken, Morrish, Kail, Goodliffe, Moseley, Robbins
Scorers: Moseley 4, Kail 2, Goodliffe
Marine: Drury, Jackson, Rankin, Crilley, Kelly, Halsall, Keir, Garvey, O'Donnell, King, Bamford
Scorer: O'Donnell
Referee: A.H. Adams (Notts)

1932-33 Amateur Cup

First Round

Badsey Rangers vs Players Athletic	1-1
Barnet vs Hampstead Town	4-0
Bishop Auckland vs Stockton	2-3
Chelmsford vs Bostall Heath	1-0
Clapton vs Cambridge Town	1-1
Erith & Belvedere vs Trowbridge	2-0
Evenwood Town vs Shildon	0-3
Hayes vs Norwich C.E.Y.M.S.	5-1
Hitchin Town vs Slough	2-2
Horsham vs H.M.S. Excellent	5-1
Maidenhead United vs Ilford	2-4
Manningham Mills vs Guiseley	1-4
Marine (Liverpool) vs Northern Nomads	7-0
Metropolitan Police vs Casuals	2-3
Nether Edge Amateurs vs Excelsior Foundry	3-1
Oxford City vs Barking	1-1
Portland United vs Kingstonian	2-2
Portrack Shamrocks vs Ferryhill Athletic	0-3
Rawmarsh Welfare vs Yorkshire Amateurs	1-1
Romford vs Leyton	1-1
St. Albans City vs Leavesden Mental Hospital	0-1
South Bank vs Willington	3-2
South Salford vs Whitehall Printeries	2-5
Stowmarket vs Bournemouth Gasworks Athletic	2-4
Uxbridge Town vs Dulwich Hamlet	1-2
Walthamstow Avenue vs Tufnell Park	1-1
Welton Rovers vs Nunhead	1-1
Weston-super-Mare vs Gorleston	3-2
Whitby United vs Stanhope	8-1
Wisbech Town vs Northampton Nomads	5-0
Woking vs London Caledonians	3-0
Wycombe Wanderers vs Wimbledon	1-2

First Round Replays

Barking vs Oxford City	0-2
Cambridge Town vs Clapton	1-5
Kingstonian vs Portland United	5-0

Leyton vs Romford   2-3*, 3-2
* abandoned during extra time
Nunhead vs Welton Rovers   7-1
Players Athletic vs Badsey Rangers   1-2
Slough vs Hitchin Town   5-1
Tufnell Park vs Walthamstow Avenue   0-1
Yorkshire Amateurs vs Rawmarsh Welfare   1-0

Second Round

Badsey Rangers vs Wisbech Town   3-1
Barnet vs Walthamstow Avenue   2-2*, 3-2
Casuals vs Nunhead   0-1
Dulwich Hamlet vs Chelmsford   5-1
Erith & Belvedere vs Ilford   0-1*, 3-2
Ferryhill Athletic vs Yorkshire Amateurs   3-0
Guiseley vs Nether Edge Amateurs   2-1
Leavesden Mental Hospital vs Horsham   6-2
Leyton vs Kingstonian   1-3
Oxford City vs Clapton   1-2
Slough vs Woking   6-1
South Bank vs Marine (Liverpool)   1-0
Stockton vs Shildon   2-0
Weston-super-Mare versus
Bournemouth Gasworks Athletic   1-1
Whitby United vs Whitehall Printeries   2-2
Wimbledon vs Hayes   3-3
* matches abandoned

Second Round Replays

Bournemouth Gasworks Athletic versus
Weston-super-Mare   1-0
Hayes vs Wimbledon   3-2
Whitehall Printeries vs Whitby United   1-1

Second Round Second Replay

Whitehall Printeries vs Whitby United   1-0
(at York)

Third Round

Erith & Belvedere vs Leavesden Mental Hospital   2-1
Ferryhill Athletic vs Stockton   1-2
Guiseley vs Bournemouth Gasworks Athletic   1-2
Hayes vs Dulwich Hamlet   1-1
Nunhead vs Clapton   0-1
Slough vs Barnet   1-2
South Bank vs Kingstonian   1-2
Whitehall Printeries vs Badsey Rangers   3-0

Third Round Replay

Dulwich Hamlet vs Hayes   4-0

Fourth Round

Bournemouth Gasworks Athletic vs Erith & Belvedere   2-0

Kingstonian vs Dulwich Hamlet   4-2
Stockton vs Barnet   2-1
Whitehall Printeries vs Clapton   8-3

Semi-Finals

Kingstonian vs Whitehall Printeries   3-0
(at West Ham)
Stockton vs Bournemouth Gasworks Athletic   2-1
(at New Cross)

Final

Kingstonian vs Stockton   1-1
(at Champion Hill, Dulwich 8 April 1933)
Attendance: 20,448

Kingstonian: Brodrick, Rassell, Urpeth, Lee, Daley,
Keene, McCarthy, Gibson, Whitehead, Macey, Okin
Scorer: Whitehead
Stockton: Newton, Thompson, Little, Foster, Butler,
Edwards, Stephenson, Smith, Coulthard, Prest, Anderson
Scorer: Anderson
Referee: J. Milward (Derby)

Final Replay

Stockton vs Kingstonian   1-4
(at Feethams, Darlington 22 April 1933)
Attendance: 16,492

Kingstonian: Brodrick, Rassell, Urpeth, Lee, Daley,
Keene, McCarthy, Gibson, Whitehead, Macey, Okin
Scorers: Gibson, Urpeth (penalty), Whitehead 2
Stockton: Newton, Thompson, Little, Foster, Pass,
Edwards, Stephenson, Smith, Coulthard, Prest, Henderson
Scorer: Coulthard
Referee: J. Milward (Derby)

1933-34 Amateur Cup

First Round

Badsey Rangers vs R.A.F. (Cranwell)   1-0
Barking vs Tufnell Park   1-1
Barnet vs Ipswich Town   4-1
1st Battalion Durham Light Infantry vs Whitby United   5-1
Bishop Auckland vs Willington   3-0
Bostall Heath vs Leyton   1-2
Casuals vs Ilford   1-1
Clapton vs Leavesden   1-2
Dulwich Hamlet vs Finchley   2-1
Hitchin Town vs Chesham United   0-0
Horsham vs Great Yarmouth Town   2-0
Keynsham vs Frome Town   1-0
London Caledonians vs Leytonstone   2-0
Marine vs Cockfield   2-1

Northern Nomads vs Evenwood Town	3-3
Oxford City vs Apsley	1-2
Poole Town vs Portland United	1-2
Portrack Shamrocks vs Stockton	1-1
St. Albans City vs Enfield	0-3
St. Neots & District vs Mount Pleasant	1-1
Slough vs Walthamstow Avenue	0-4
South Bank vs Guiseley	2-0
South Hetton Colliery vs W.D.U. (Liverpool)	2-1
Sutton United vs Erith & Belvedere	3-2
Weston-super-Mare versus	
Bournemouth Gasworks Athletic	0-0
Metropolitan Police vs Gorleston	2-1
MoorGreen vs Yorkshire Amateurs	1-1
Morris Motors (Cowley) vs Maidenhead	1-2
Nether Edge Amateurs vs Rawmarsh Welfare	2-5
Whitehall Printeries vs Ferryhill Athletic	0-1
Wimbledon vs Woking	2-1
Wycombe Wanderers vs Kingstonian	0-1

First Round Replays

Barking vs Tufnell Park	1-2
Bournemouth Gasworks Athletic versus	
Weston-super-Mare	4-0
Chesham United vs Hitchin Town	6-3
Evenwood Town vs Northern Nomads	4-4
Ilford vs Casuals	0-3
Mount Pleasant vs St. Neots & District	5-3
Stockton vs Portrack Shamrocks	0-1
Yorkshire Amateurs vs Moor Green	2-0

First Round Second Replay

Evenwood Town vs Northern Nomads	2-2
(at Evenwood)	

First Round Third Replay

Evenwood Town vs Northern Nomads	4-0
(at Evenwood)	

Second Round

Apsley vs Sutton United	1-4
Badsey Rangers vs Portrack Shamrocks	1-0
Barnet vs Horsham	4-2
Bishop Auckland vs Yorkshire Amateurs	0-1
Casuals vs Tufnell Park	2-1
Chesham United vs Maidenhead	7-1
Dulwich Hamlet vs Walthamstow Avenue	3-2
Enfield vs Leyton	1-1
Evenwood Town vs 1st Battalion Durham Light Infantry	2-1
Kingstonian vs Wimbledon	1-1
London Caledonians vs Leavesden	2-0
Metropolitan Police vs Keynsham	4-3
Portland United vs Bournemouth Gasworks Athletic	0-5

Rawmarsh Welfare vs Mount Pleasant	5-1
South Bank vs Marine	3-0
South Hetton Colliery vs Ferryhill Athletic	2-2

Second Round Replays

Ferryhill Athletic vs South Hetton Colliery	0-3
Leyton vs Enfield	1-1
Wimbledon vs Kingstonian	3-0

Second Round Second Replay

Leyton vs Enfield	3-0
(at Ilford)	

Third Round

Badsey Rangers vs Chesham United	1-3
Barnet vs Wimbledon	3-1
Bournemouth Gasworks Athletic vs Casuals	1-5
Evenwood Town vs South Bank	3-3*
* abandoned during extra time	
London Caledonians vs Rawmarsh Welfare	2-0
Metropolitan Police vs Yorkshire Amateurs	4-1
South Hetton Colliery vs Leyton	1-3
Sutton United vs Dulwich Hamlet	1-3

Third Round Replay

South Bank vs Evenwood Town	2-1

Fourth Round

Barnet vs London Caledonians	2-0
Casuals vs Dulwich Hamlet	1-2
Metropolitan Police vs Chesham United	4-0
South Bank vs Leyton	0-1

Semi-Finals

Dulwich Hamlet vs Metropolitan Police	2-0
(at Wimbledon)	
Leyton vs Barnet	2-0
(at Ilford)	

Final

Leyton vs Dulwich Hamlet	1-2
(at Upton Park, London 21 April 1934)	

Attendance: 33,000

Dulwich Hamlet: Cummings, Hugo, Robins, Murray, Hamer, Toser, Morrish, Miller, Goodliffe, Benka, Court
Scorers: Robbins, Court
Leyton: Holding, Loveday, E. Caesar, Richardson, Mercer, Collins, Gibbins, Skeels, Coates, Davis
Scorer: Davis
Referee: J.M. Wiltshire (Dorset)

1934-35 Amateur Cup

First Round

Aylesbury United vs Sutton United	0-1
Barnet vs Lowestoft Town	3-0
Bishop Auckland vs Evenwood Town	3-0
Bournemouth Gasworks Athletic vs Banbury Spencer	2-1
Bromley vs Woking	2-1
Cambridge Town vs St. Neots & District	1-1
Chesham United vs Harwich & Parkeston	2-0
Dulwich Hamlet vs Horsham	3-2
Farsley Celtic vs Whitehall Printeries	3-0
Gloucester City vs Frome Town	0-3
Golders Green vs Enfield	1-2
Grangetown St. Mary's vs Ferryhill Athletic	2-1
Great Yarmouth Town vs Walthamstow Avenue	1-3
Guiseley vs Humber United	3-2
Hastings & St. Leonards vs Wycombe Wanderers	1-1
Hitchin Town vs Finchley	1-1
H.M.S. Victory vs Portland United	6-1
Ibstock Penistone Rovers vs Mount Pleasant	4-2
Ilford vs London Caledonians	2-2
Leyton vs Gorleston	2-1
Leytonstone vs Leavesden	1-0
Maidenhead United vs Nunhead	3-1
Metropolitan Police vs Kingstonian	0-3
Moor Green vs Jack Mould's Athletic	2-1
Northern Nomads vs Marine	4-0
Oxford City vs Casuals	0-1
Rawmarsh Welfare vs Yorkshire Amateurs	0-3
Romford vs Tufnell Park	7-0
Shildon vs Witton Park Institute	3-0
South Bank vs Stockton	1-0
Stanley United vs Willington	1-0
Wimbledon vs Epsom Town	2-0

First Round Replays

Finchley vs Hitchin Town	0-1
London Caledonians vs Ilford	1-1
St. Neots & District vs Cambridge Town	1-5
Wycombe Wanderers vs Hastings & St. Leonards	4-2

First Round Second Replay

London Caledonians vs Ilford (at Dulwich)	1-0

Second Round

Barnet vs London Caledonians	2-3
Bishop Auckland vs Grangetown St. Mary's	4-0
Bromley vs Wycombe Wanderers	2-1
Chesham United vs Wimbledon	0-2
Enfield vs Maidenhead United	4-1
Farsley Celtic vs Northern Nomads	2-0
Frome Town vs Casuals	2-4
Guiseley vs Moor Green	4-3
Hitchin Town vs Sutton United	4-2
Ibstock Penistone Rovers vs Cambridge Town	2-3
Kingstonian vs Bournemouth Gasworks Athletic	4-1
Leyton vs Romford	2-3
Leytonstone vs H.M.S. Victory	0-0
Stanley United vs South Bank	0-2
Walthamstow Avenue vs Dulwich Hamlet	0-1
Yorkshire Amateurs vs Shildon	1-0

Second Round Replay

H.M.S. Victory vs Leytonstone	0-0

Second Round Second Replay

H.M.S. Victory vs Leytonstone (at Kingstonian)	3-3

Second Round Third Replay

H.M.S. Victory vs Leytonstone (at Kingstonian)	5-3*

* a further replay was ordered after H.M.S. Victory used an ineligible player

Second Round Fourth Replay

H.M.S. Victory vs Leytonstone (at Wimbledon)	2-0

Third Round

Bishop Auckland vs Farsley Celtic	11-1
Dulwich Hamlet vs London Caledonians	3-0
Enfield vs South Bank	3-0
Guiseley vs Cambridge Town	3-4
Hitchin Town vs Casuals	0-1
Kingstonian vs Yorkshire Amateurs	3-0
Romford vs Bromley	1-2
Wimbledon vs H.M.S. Victory	3-0

Fourth Round

Bishop Auckland vs Casuals	1-0
Bromley vs Wimbledon	1-2
Dulwich Hamlet vs Kingstonian	1-0
Enfield vs Cambridge Town	4-2

Semi-Finals

Bishop Auckland vs Dulwich Hamlet (at Middlesbrough)	3-0
Wimbledon vs Enfield (at Dulwich Hamlet)	1-0

Final

Bishop Auckland vs Wimbledon	0-0

(at Middlesbrough 13 April 1935)

Attendance: 20,000

Bishop Auckland: Hopps, Minton, Scott, Birbeck, Staughan, Shield, Dodds, Bryan, Wilson, Stephenson, Hogg
Wimbledon: Irish, Goodchild, Balkwill, Wright, Bridge, Reeves, Batchelor, Barnes, Dowden, Turner, Smith
Referee: Dr. A.W. Barton (A.F.A.)

Final Replay

Wimbledon vs Bishop Auckland	1-2

(at Stamford Bridge, London 20 April 1935)

Attendance: 30,000

Bishop Auckland: Hopps, Minton, Scott, Birbeck, Staughan, Shield, Dodds, Bryan, Wilson, Stephenson, Hogg
Scorers: Wilson, Bryan
Wimbledon: Irish, Goodchild, Balkwill, Wright, Bridge, Reeves, Smith, Barnes, Dowden, Turner, Zenthon
Scorer: Dowden
Referee: Dr. A.W. Barton (A.F.A.)

1935-36 Amateur Cup

First Round

Barking vs Chesham United	6-1
Cambridge Town vs Chatteris Engineers	3-2
Casuals vs Horsham	4-1
Clapton vs Ilford	1-5
Cockfield vs 4th Battalion Royal Tank Corps	2-2
Dulwich Hamlet vs Metropolitan Police	5-1
Farsley Celtic vs Northern Nomads	3-2
Golders Green vs Leyton	2-2
Gosport vs Bournemouth Gasworks Athletic	2-1
Grangetown St. Mary's vs Willington	0-1
Guiseley vs Yorkshire Amateurs	4-2
Heaton Stannington vs Pease & Partners	7-3
Hitchin Town vs Enfield	1-2
H.M.S. Victory vs St. Pancras (Bristol)	4-1
I.C.I. Alkali vs Whitehall Printeries	4-3
Ipswich Town vs Kings Lynn	6-1
Leavesden vs Kingstonian	2-2
Leytonstone vs London Caledonians	0-1
Maidenhead United vs R.A.M.C. (Aldershot)	4-4
Maidstone United vs Wimbledon	3-2
Marine (Liverpool) vs Norton Woodseats	2-1
Moor Green vs Badsey Rangers	1-2
Morris Motors (Coventry) vs R.A.F. (Cranwell)	1-1
Oxford City vs Sutton United	1-1
Portland United vs Frome Town	2-1
Romford vs Barnet	6-2

Shildon vs Bishop Auckland	1-1
Stockton vs South Bank	2-0
Uxbridge Town vs Tufnell Park	4-1
Walthamstow Avenue vs Southall	3-3
Worthing vs Bromley	3-2
Wycombe Wanderers vs Nunhead	2-1

First Round Replays

4th Battalion Royal Tank Corps vs Cockfield	0-1
Bishop Auckland vs Shildon	2-1
Kingstonian vs Leavesden	7-0
Leyton vs Golders Green	0-3
R.A.F. (Cranwell) vs Morris Motors (Coventry)	1-2
R.A.M.C. (Aldershot) vs Maidenhead United	1-5
Southall vs Walthamstow Avenue	5-2
Sutton United vs Oxford City	4-1

Second Round

Barking vs Golders Green	1-2
Bishop Auckland vs Willington	2-1
Cambridge Town vs Badsey Rangers	3-4
Cockfield vs Guiseley	6-2
Dulwich Hamlet vs Gosport	11-0
Enfield vs Uxbridge Town	1-1
Farsley Celtic vs Marine (Liverpool)	1-8
H.M.S. Victory vs Maidenhead United	1-3
I.C.I. Alkali vs Morris Motors (Coventry)	6-2
Ilford vs Portland United	6-0
Kingstonian vs Ipswich Town	4-2
London Caledonians vs Sutton United	0-2
Maidstone United vs Romford	0-7
Southall vs Worthing	9-1
Stockton vs Heaton Stannington	4-2
Wycombe Wanderers vs Casuals	0-2

Second Round Replay

Uxbridge Town vs Enfield	2-4

Third Round

Casuals vs Bishop Auckland	4-0
Cockfield vs Kingstonian	4-2
I.C.I. Alkali vs Golders Green	4-2
Ilford vs Enfield	5-0
Maidenhead United vs Badsey Rangers	3-1
Romford vs Dulwich Hamlet	4-2
Southall vs Marine (Liverpool)	7-0
Stockton vs Sutton United	1-2

Fourth Round

Casuals vs I.C.I. Alkali	3-0
Ilford vs Cockfield	2-2
Maidenhead United vs Southall	1-0
Romford vs Sutton United	4-1

Fourth Round Replay

Cockfield vs Ilford   3-7

Semi-Finals

Casuals vs Romford   3-2
(at Dulwich Hamlet)
Ilford vs Maidenhead United   4-1
(at West Ham)

Final

Casuals vs Ilford   1-1
(at Selhurst Park, London 18 April 1936)
Attendance: 25,064

Casuals: Huddle, Whewell, Evans, Allen, Joy, Couchman, Shearer, Fabian, Clements, Webster, Riley
Scorer: Riley
Ilford: Tietjon, Holmes, Hayes, Male, Myers, Craymer, Gilderson, Manley, Watts, Halcrow, Braund
Scorer: Braund
Referee: C.E. Argent (Herts)

Final Replay

Ilford vs Casuals   0-2
(at Upton Park, London 2 May 1936)
Attendance: 27,000

Casuals: Huddle, Whewell, Evans, Allen, Joy, Couchman, Shearer, Fabian, Clements, Webster, Riley
Scorers: Shearer, Webster
Ilford: Tietjon, Holmes, Hayes, Male, Myers, Craymer, Gilderson, Manley, Watts, Halcrow, Braund
Referee: C.E. Argent (Herts)

1936-37 Amateur Cup

First Round

Anglo (Purfleet) vs Barking	3-2
Aylesford Paper Mills vs Wimbledon	3-1
Barnet vs Lowestoft Town	4-2
Boldmere St. Michael's vs Cambridge Town	3-0
Bromley vs Horsham	3-2
Casuals vs Oxford City	4-1
Clapton vs H.M.S. Victory	8-0
Crittall's Athletic vs Walthamstow Avenue	2-4
Enfield vs Southall	2-5
Evenwood Town vs South Bank	1-2
Gorleston vs Wycombe Wanderers	0-0
Guiseley vs South Bank East End	3-3
Hastings & St. Leonards versus Bournemouth Gasworks Athletic	0-4
Hayes vs Walton-on-Thames	3-0

Heaton Stannington vs Shildon	3-1
Hitchin Town vs Dulwich Hamlet	2-4
I.C.I. Alkali vs Marine	2-1
Leyton vs Worthing	8-4
London Paper Mills vs Golders Green	3-2
Maidenhead United vs Sutton United	1-3
Norton Woodseats vs Badsey Rangers	5-2
Nunhead vs Kingstonian	4-1
Portland United vs Harwich & Parkeston	2-0
R.A.F. (Cranwell) vs Moor Green	0-1
Redhill vs Metropolitan Police	0-2
Romford vs London Caledonians	3-0
St. Pancras (Knowle) vs Uxbridge	4-5
Stockton vs Cockfield	3-1
Tufnell Park vs Ilford	3-1
Wealdstone vs Chesham United	4-0
Willington vs Bishop Auckland	3-4
Yorkshire Amateurs vs Farsley Celtic	1-1

First Round Replays

Farsley Celtic vs Yorkshire Amateurs	0-1
South Bank East End vs Guiseley	5-2
Wycombe Wanderers vs Gorleston	3-2

Second Round

Aylesford Paper Mills vs London Paper Mills	3-5
Bishop Auckland vs South Bank East End	7-0
Bromley vs Tufnell Park	5-1
Dulwich Hamlet vs Casuals	1-0
Hayes vs Anglo (Purfleet)	4-1
Leyton vs Clapton	7-2
Metropolitan Police versus Bournemouth Gasworks Athletic	1-2
Moor Green vs Boldmere St. Michael's	6-0
Norton Woodseats vs I.C.I. Alkali	0-4
Romford vs Portland United	4-2
South Bank vs Yorkshire Amateurs	2-5
Stockton vs Heaton Stannington	5-3
Sutton United vs Barnet	2-1
Uxbridge vs Wealdstone	1-3
Walthamstow Avenue vs Southall	6-1
Wycombe Wanderers vs Nunhead	4-2

Third Round

Bromley vs Bournemouth Gasworks Athletic	4-0
Hayes vs I.C.I. Alkali	2-3
London Paper Mills vs Leyton	0-1
Moor Green vs Bishop Auckland	0-2
Romford vs Sutton United	3-4
Stockton vs Wycombe Wanderers	4-1
Walthamstow Avenue vs Yorkshire Amateurs	3-1
Wealdstone vs Dulwich Hamlet	1-1

Third Round Replay

Dulwich Hamlet vs Wealdstone	4-0

Fourth Round

Bromley vs Stockton	4-1
Leyton vs Bishop Auckland	3-2
Sutton United vs I.C.I. Alkali	3-2
Walthamstow Avenue vs Dulwich Hamlet	1-2

Semi-Finals

Dulwich Hamlet vs Bromley	3-1
(at Selhurst Park)	
Leyton vs Sutton United	1-1
(at Ilford)	

Semi-Final Replay

Sutton United vs Leyton	1-2
(at Wimbledon)	

Final

Leyton vs Dulwich Hamlet	0-2
(at Upton Park, London 7 April 1937)	

Attendance: 33,516

Dulwich Hamlet: Hill, Weymouth, Robbins, Murray, Hugo, Toser, Morrish, Anderson, Wright, Ingleton, Ball
Scorer: Moorish 2
Leyton: Self, Gentry, Clark, Hunt, Preston, Burns, Smith, Leek, Avery, Boatwright, Camerson
Referee: F/Sgt F. Warner (R.A.F.)

1937-38 Amateur Cup

First Round

Aylesford Paper Mills vs Enfield	2-2
Barnet vs Metropolitan Police	2-0
Boldmere St. Michael's vs Badsey Rangers	1-1
Bournemouth Gasworks Athletic vs Leytonstone	0-1
Crittall's Athletic vs Tooting & Mitcham United	4-2
Dulwich Hamlet vs Woking	7-0
Erith & Belvedere vs Worthing	3-0
Eton Manor vs Bromley	0-1
Finchley vs Casuals	4-1
Golders Green vs Barking	2-1
Guiseley vs Farsley Celtic	0-7
Harwich & Parkeston vs Portsmouth Gasworks	6-3
Hayes vs Leyton	4-5
Heaton Stannington vs Bishop Auckland	3-2
Holt United vs Oxford City	2-0
Horsham vs London Caledonians	4-1
I.C.I. Alkali vs Yorkshire Amateurs	0-1

Kingstonian vs Waterlows	3-2
Maidenhead United vs Wimbledon	3-1
Marine vs Urmston	3-2
Moor Green vs Northern Nomads	2-1
Newmarket Town vs Cambridge Town	1-3
Nunhead vs Walthamstow Avenue	1-6
Portland United vs Wycombe Wanderers	1-4
Purton vs Lowestoft Town	0-2
Romford vs Chesham United	4-2
Shildon vs South Bank	3-1
Southall vs Ilford	1-5
South Bank East End vs Ferryhill Athletic	1-4
Sutton United vs Wealdstone	2-0
Uxbridge vs Clapton	1-2
Willington vs Stockton	1-4

First Round Replays

Badsey Rangers vs Boldmere St. Michael's	2-3
Enfield vs Aylesford Paper Mills	1-2

Second Round

Aylesford Paper Mills vs Wycombe Wanderers	4-2
Boldmere St. Michael's vs Marine	2-2
Bromley vs Clapton	4-2
Dulwich Hamlet vs Crittall's Athletic	3-1
Erith & Belvedere vs Maidenhead United	1-0
Ferryhill Athletic vs Stockton	0-2
Finchley vs Harwich & Parkeston	0-2
Golders Green vs Leyton	0-2
Heaton Stannington vs Shildon	2-3
Holt United vs Barnet	0-2
Horsham vs Kingstonian	1-1
Ilford vs Lowestoft Town	4-2
Moor Green vs Cambridge Town	2-5
Sutton United vs Leytonstone	1-1
Walthamstow Avenue vs Romford	1-1
Yorkshire Amateurs vs Farsley Celtic	2-0

Second Round Replays

Kingstonian vs Horsham	2-1
Leytonstone vs Sutton United	3-1
Marine vs Boldmere St. Michael's	3-2
Romford vs Walthamstow Avenue	4-1

Third Round

Aylesford Paper Mills vs Cambridge Town	2-2
Barnet vs Stockton	3-0
Erith & Belvedere vs Leytonstone	2-2
Ilford vs Dulwich Hamlet	2-3
Kingstonian vs Shildon	1-2
Leyton vs Romford	2-4
Marine vs Harwich & Parkeston	2-3
Yorkshire Amateurs vs Bromley	1-2

Third Round Replays

Cambridge Town vs Aylesford Paper Mills	1-3
Leytonstone vs Erith & Belvedere	1-1

Third Round Second Replay

Erith & Belvedere vs Leytonstone	3-1
(at Dulwich Hamlet)	

Fourth Round

Bromley vs Shildon	4-1
Dulwich Hamlet vs Barnet	1-3
Erith & Belvedere vs Aylesford Paper Mills	4-2
Harwich & Parkeston vs Romford	0-2

Semi-Finals

Bromley vs Barnet	3-2
(at Dulwich Hamlet)	
Romford vs Erith & Belvedere	2-2
(at Clapton Orient)	

Semi-Final Replay

Erith & Belvedere vs Romford	4-2
(at Selhurst Park)	

Final

Bromley vs Erith & Belvedere	1-0
(at The Den, Millwall 23 April 1938)	

Attendance: 33,000

Bromley: Bartaby, Gray, Clark, Wade, Weeks, Barnes, Thomas, Stroud, Brown, Holbrook, Reece
Scorer: Stroud
Erith & Belvedere: Gibbs, Little, O'Hara, Smee, Fuller, Bennett, Young, Scott, Southcombe, Beale, Sanders
Referee: J.H. Lockton (Surrey)

1938-39 Amateur Cup

First Round

Boldmere St. Michael's vs Moor Green	2-4
Cambridge Town vs Jack Mould's Athletic	2-1
Chesham United vs Enfield	1-1
Chippenham Town vs Gorleston	1-3
Clapton vs Maidenhead United	2-2
Dulwich Hamlet vs Leytonstone	1-3
Erith & Belvedere vs Barking	1-1
Eton Manor vs Bromley	2-4
Farsley Celtic vs Yorkshire Amateurs	1-4
Ferguson Pailin vs Marine (Liverpool)	0-2
Harwich & Parkeston vs Casuals	1-9
Hastings & St. Leonards vs Leavesden	4-1
Hitchin Town vs Tooting & Mitcham United	1-1
I.C.I. Alkali vs Rawmarsh Welfare	2-0
Ilford vs London Paper Mills	6-3
Kingstonian vs Ford Sports	3-1
Leyton vs Romford	3-0
London Caledonians vs Golders Green	0-0
Norton Woodseats vs Badsey Rangers	9-0
Portland United vs Sutton United	0-1
R.A.S.C. (Aldershot) vs Barnet	3-2
St. Albans City vs Howards Heath	2-1
Shildon vs Evenwood Town	7-0
Southall vs Hounslow Town	2-2
South Bank vs Guiseley	2-1
Southwick vs Hayes	3-1
Wallsend St. Luke's vs Bishop Auckland	0-1
Walthamstow Avenue vs Wealdstone	4-2
Willington vs Stockton	2-1
Wimbledon vs Bournemouth Gasworks Athletic	3-3
Woking vs Tufnell Park	2-1
Wycombe Wanderers vs Slough	1-5

First Round Replays

Barking vs Erith & Belvedere	1-0
Bournemouth Gasworks Athletic vs Wimbledon	0-1
Enfield vs Chesham United	7-0
Golders Green vs London Caledonians	2-0
Hounslow Town vs Southall	1-1
Maidenhead United vs Clapton	1-0
Tooting and Mitcham United vs Hitchin Town	3-1

First Round Second Replay

Southall vs Hounslow Town	2-2
(at Hayes)	

First Round Third Replay

Hounslow Town vs Southall	2-3
(at Q.P.R.)	

Second Round

Bromley vs Southall	4-1
Cambridge Town vs Marine (Liverpool)	2-1
Golders Green vs Southwick	2-1
Hastings & St. Leonards vs Barking	4-3
Kingstonian vs Gorleston	5-3
Leyton vs Casuals	1-0
Moor Green vs Yorkshire Amateurs	4-0
Norton Woodseats vs I.C.I. Alkali	2-1
R.A.S.C. (Aldershot) vs Enfield	1-3
Slough vs St. Albans City	0-3
South Bank vs Bishop Auckland	1-7
Sutton United vs Maidenhead United	4-1
Tooting & Mitcham United vs Leytonstone	1-2
Walthamstow Avenue vs Ilford	2-3

Willington vs Shildon	2-0
Woking vs Wimbledon	1-3

Third Round

Bishop Auckland vs Leyton	2-0
Cambridge Town vs Ilford	0-2
Kingstonian vs Hastings & St. Leonards	4-0
Leytonstone vs Bromley	1-1
Norton Woodseats vs Wimbledon	3-1
St. Albans City vs Enfield	2-1
Sutton United vs Golders Green	4-2
Willington vs Moor Green	1-0

Third Round Replay

Bromley vs Leytonstone	1-2

Fourth Round

Bishop Auckland vs Ilford	3-1
St. Albans City vs Norton Woodseats	2-4
Sutton United vs Leytonstone	0-2
Willington vs Kingstonian	1-0

Semi-Finals

Leytonstone vs Bishop Auckland	0-0
(at Wimbledon)	
Willington vs Norton Woodseats	1-0
(at Middlesbrough)	

Semi-Final Replay

Bishop Auckland vs Leytonstone	2-1
(at Darlington)	

Final

Bishop Auckland vs Willington	3-0
(at Roker Park, Sunderland 22 April 1939)	

Attendance: 25,064

Bishop Auckland: Washington, Kirtley, Humble, Wanless, Straughan, Paisley, Twigg, Wensley, Slee, Evans, Young
Scorer: Wensley 3
Willington: Coe, Cooper, Etheridge, Hardy, Lumby, Hindmarsh, Mitchell, Pratt, McLean, Davidson, Elliott
Referee: G. Hewitt (Liverpool)

1945-46 Amateur Cup

First Round

Abbey United vs Hitchin Town	3-5
Bishop Auckland vs Ferguson Pailin	7-1
Bournemouth Gasworks vs Totton	2-5
Bromley vs Barking	1-0
Chippenham Town vs Slough United	1-5
Clapton vs Enfield	2-1
Crook Colliery Welfare vs Evenwood Town	5-3
Erith & Belvedere vs Sutton United	2-2
Golders Green vs Ford Sports	2-1
Guiseley vs Billingham Synthonia	4-3
Hastings & St. Leonards vs Eastbourne	1-2
Hayes vs Wealdstone	3-0
Kings Lynn vs Cambridge Town	4-1
Kingstonian vs Wycombe Wanderers	1-1
Leyton vs Tufnell Park	4-0
Marine (Crosby) vs Basford United	5-2
Metropolitan Police vs Letchworth Town	4-0
Moor Green vs Bournville Athletic	2-0
Norton Woodseats vs I.C.I Alkali	6-1
Oxford City vs Maidenhead United	5-2
Raleigh Athletic vs Rawmarsh Welfare	2-5
Romford vs Leytonstone	0-0
St. Albans City vs Ilford	0-3
Southall vs Grays Athletic	3-1
South Bank vs Yorkshire Amateurs	3-0
Stanley United vs Shildon	9-0
Walthamstow Avenue vs Dulwich Hamlet	3-0
Walton & Hersham vs Corinthian Casuals	3-2
Willington vs Ferryhill Athletic	3-3*
* abandoned during extra time	
Wimbledon vs Crittall Athletic	3-1
Woking vs Finchley	2-1
Wood Green Town vs Barnet	3-4

First Round Replays

Leytonstone vs Romford	3-5
Sutton United vs Erith & Belvedere	2-4
Willington vs Ferryhill Athletic	1-3
Wycombe Wanderers vs Kingstonian	10-1

Second Round

Barnet vs Walthamstow Avenue	4-0
Bishop Auckland vs Stanley United	3-0
Clapton vs Erith & Belvedere	1-2
Eastbourne vs Totton	5-2
Ferryhill Athletic vs Crook Colliery Welfare	5-1
Golders Green vs Leyton	1-3
Hayes vs Bromley	0-4
Hitchin Town vs Kings Lynn	5-3
Ilford vs Metropolitan Police	5-1
Marine (Crosby) vs Rawmarsh Welfare	4-2
Moor Green vs Norton Woodseats	4-1
Oxford City vs Slough United	2-3
Southall vs Romford	4-2
South Bank vs Guiseley	3-1
Wimbledon vs Woking	5-2
Wycombe Wanderers vs Walthamstow Avenue	1-1

Second Round Replay

Walthamstow Avenue vs Wycombe Wanderers	7-5

Third Round

Bromley vs Walthamstow Avenue	0-0
Eastbourne vs Erith & Belvedere	2-3
Hitchin Town vs Barnet	2-5
Leyton vs Southall	2-4
Marine (Crosby) vs Ferryhill Athletic	4-1
Moor Green vs Slough United	2-1
South Bank vs Bishop Auckland	1-3
Wimbledon vs Ilford	1-2

Third Round Replay

Walthamstow Avenue vs Bromley	2-1

Fourth Round

Barnet vs Southall	4-3
Bishop Auckland vs Moor Green	4-1
Ilford vs Walthamstow Avenue	2-3
Marine (Crosby) vs Erith & Belvedere	2-1

Semi-Finals

Barnet vs Marine (Crosby)	1-0
(at Dulwich Hamlet)	
Bishop Auckland vs Walthamstow Avenue	2-1
(at Darlington)	

Final

Barnet vs Bishop Auckland	3-2
(at Stamford Bridge 20 April 1946)	

Attendance: 53,832

Barnet: Powell, Wheeler, Bunker, Gerrans, Pullen, Weightman, Jordan, Kelleher, Phipps, Finch, Reilly
Scorers: Reilly, Phipps, Kelleher
Bishop Auckland: Washington, Humble, Farrer, Longstaff, Hadfield, Fairs, Shergold, Richardson, Teasdale, Tait, Anderson
Scorers: Teasdale 2
Referee: C.J. Barrick (Northants)

1946-47 Amateur Cup

First Round

Barking vs Hayes	1-2
Barnet vs Woolwich Polytechnic	3-0
Bournville Athletic vs Coalville Town Amateurs	1-5
Cambridge Town vs Hitchin Town	2-1
Crook Colliery Welfare vs Penrith	0-3
Corinthian Casuals vs Bromley	1-3
Dulwich Hamlet vs Leyton	4-1
Eastbourne vs Wimbledon	2-4
Ferryhill Athletic vs Heaton Stannington	3-2
Finchley vs Metropolitan Police	4-4
Gosport Borough Athletic vs Dorchester Town	6-1
Grays Athletic vs Tooting & Mitcham United	3-1
Hastings & St. Leonards vs Woking	1-3
Hounslow Town vs Wealdstone	3-1
Ilford vs Hendon	2-1
Kingstonian vs Crittall Athletic	4-0
Maidstone United vs Sutton United	2-1
Marine (Crosby) vs I.C.I. Alkali	3-0
Moor Green vs Basford United	2-1
Peasedown Miners Welfare versus	
Bournemouth Gasworks Athletic	2-1
Rawmarsh Welfare vs Guiseley	3-5
Romford vs Clapton	0-3
Shildon vs Bishop Auckland	1-1
Southall vs Walton & Hersham	1-2
Tow Law Town vs Stanley United	4-0
Tufnell Park vs Leavesden United	1-6
Vauxhall Motors vs Lowestoft Town	0-1
Walthamstow Avenue vs Leytonstone	2-3
Willington vs South Bank	2-1
Wood Green Town vs Tilbury	1-3
Wycombe Wanderers vs Enfield	3-3
Yorkshire Amateurs vs Norton Woodseats	1-2

First Round Replays

Bishop Auckland vs Shildon	4-2
Enfield vs Wycombe Wanderers	5-2
Metropolitan Police vs Finchley	2-0

Second Round

Bishop Auckland vs Marine (Crosby)	4-0
Bromley vs Kingstonian	5-1
Dulwich Hamlet vs Grays Athletic	3-3
Enfield vs Walton & Hersham	3-0
Guiseley vs Ferryhill Athletic	2-4
Hayes vs Clapton	4-2
Hounslow Town vs Maidstone United	3-0
Ilford vs Barnet	0-3
Leavesden Hospital vs Peasedown Miners Welfare	1-0
Leytonstone vs Woking	3-1
Lowestoft Town vs Gosport Borough Athletic	3-1
Metropolitan Police vs Tilbury	0-1
Norton Woodseats vs Moor Green	4-0
Tow Law Town vs Coalville Town Amateurs	3-2
Willington vs Penrith	5-3
Wimbledon vs Cambridge Town	2-1

Second Round Replay

Grays Athletic vs Dulwich Hamlet	1-0

Third Round

Barnet vs Hounslow Town	3-1
Ferryhill Athletic vs Bromley	3-4
Hayes vs Leytonstone	0-0
Lowestoft Town vs Tow Law Town	1-0
Norton Woodseats vs Enfield	2-3
Tilbury vs Leavesden Hospital	4-1
Willington vs Bishop Auckland	1-6
Wimbledon vs Grays Athletic	3-0

Third Round Replay

Leytonstone vs Hayes	2-1

Fourth Round

Barnet vs Lowestoft Town	5-1
Bishop Auckland vs Bromley	5-1
Leytonstone vs Enfield	3-1
Wimbledon vs Tilbury	8-4

Semi-Finals

Leytonstone vs Barnet	2-1
(at Brentford)	
Wimbledon vs Bishop Auckland	4-2
(at Dulwich Hamlet)	

Final

Leytonstone vs Wimbledon	2-1

(at Highbury, London 19 April 1947)

Attendance: 47,000

Leytonstone: Jarvis, Nicholls, Childs, Banham, Lister, Kavanagh, Smith, Noble, Groves, Bunce, Crowe
Scorers: Noble, Smith
Wimbledon: Haydock, Wallis, Cousins, Magill, Clark, Lemmer, Nash, Stannard, Edelston, Head, Laker
Scorer: Stannard
Referee: W. Ling (Cambs)

1947-48 Amateur Cup

First Round

Abbey United vs Cambridge Town	0-1
Bishop Auckland vs Penrith	7-3
Boldmere St. Michael's vs Coalville Town Amateurs	7-0
Bromley vs Wimbledon	3-4
Clapton vs Dulwich Hamlet	1-2
Earle vs Norton Woodseats	2-2
East Tanfield C.W. vs Tow Law Town	2-1
Erith & Belvedere vs Leytonstone	0-1
Ferryhill Athletic vs South Bank	2-0
Gorleston vs Lowestoft Town	3-2

Gosport Borough Athletic vs Worthing	2-1
Grays Athletic vs Barnet	3-3
Guiseley vs Yorkshire Amateurs	4-5
Hastings & St. Leonards vs Romford	4-1
Hayes vs St. Albans City	1-3
Ilford vs Hounslow Town	4-1
Kingstonian vs Hendon	1-2
Letchworth Town vs Huntley & Palmers	4-1
Maidstone United vs Walton & Hersham	0-5
Metropolitan Police vs Leavesden Hospital	3-2
Moor Green vs Bournville Athletic	2-1
Poole Town vs Totton	6-1
Portsmouth Electricity vs St. Austell	6-2
Raleigh Athletic vs Marine (Crosby)	1-10
Shildon vs Willington	5-2
Stanley United vs Billingham Synthonia	0-0
3rd Battalion R.A.S.C. vs Barking	1-4
Tilbury vs West Thurrock Athletic	2-0
Tooting & Mitcham United vs Enfield	2-0
Wealdstone vs Sutton United	0-0
Wolverton Town vs Vauxhall Motors	2-4
Wycombe Wanderers vs Walthamstow Avenue	2-1

First Round Replays

Barnet vs Grays Athletic	4-1
Billingham Synthonia vs Stanley United	0-1
Norton Woodseats vs Earle	8-1
Sutton United vs Wealdstone	3-4

Second Round

Barnet vs Metropolitan Police	7-2
Dulwich Hamlet vs Tilbury	6-1
East Tanfield C.W. vs Moor Green	2-1*, 2-3
* match abandoned	
Ferryhill Athletic vs Bishop Auckland	0-6
Hastings & St. Leonards vs Cambridge Town	0-5
Hendon vs Poole Town	3-1
Ilford vs Vauxhall Motors	2-1
Letchworth Town vs Gosport Borough Athletic	0-1
Norton Woodseats vs Marine (Crosby)	3-2
Portsmouth Electricity vs Barking	2-3
St. Albans City vs Wycombe Wanderers	3-3
Shildon vs Boldmere St. Michael's	1-4
Stanley United vs Yorkshire Amateurs	1-4
Tooting & Mitcham United vs Leytonstone	0-2
Walton & Hersham vs Gorleston	2-1
Wimbledon vs Wealdstone	0-1

Second Round Replay

Wycombe Wanderers vs St. Albans City	2-1

Third Round

Barnet vs Cambridge Town	6-0

Bishop Auckland vs Norton Woodseats	5-0
Boldmere St. Michael's vs Gosport Borough Athletic	4-1
Hendon vs Barking	2-2
Ilford vs Wycombe Wanderers	2-3
Moor Green vs Walton & Hersham	2-1
Wealdstone vs Leytonstone	0-1
Yorkshire Amateurs vs Dulwich Hamlet	2-3

Third Round Replay

Barking vs Hendon	0-3*, 2-3†

* match abandoned   † replay played at Highbury

Fourth Round

Barnet vs Dulwich Hamlet	2-1
Bishop Auckland vs Wycombe Wanderers	6-2
Boldmere St. Michael's vs Moor Green	1-0
Hendon vs Leytonstone	1-4

Semi-Finals

Barnet vs Boldmere St. Michael's	2-0
(at Highbury)	
Bishop Auckland vs Leytonstone	0-5
(at Middlesbrough)	

Final

Leytonstone vs Barnet	1-0
(at Stamford Bridge 17 April 1948)	

Attendance: 59,605

Leytonstone: Jarvis, Nicholls, Childs, Wilson, Paviour, Kavanagh, Smith, Noble, Groves, Bunce, Joseph
Scorer: Groves
Barnet: Powell, Wheeler, Hawkins, Gerrans, Leek, Hawkes, Haskow, Kelleher, Phipps, Mott, Finch
Referee: F. White (Lancashire)

1948-49 Amateur Cup

First Round

Billingham Synthonia vs Penrith	5-2
Bournville Athletic vs Brentwood & Warley	0-3
Bromley vs Maidenhead United	3-0
Cambridge Town vs Barnet	2-1
Edgware Town vs Briggs Sports	2-1
Erith & Belvedere vs Hounslow Town	3-1
Ferryhill Athletic vs Stork	3-2
Finchley vs Histon Institute	2-0
Gosport Borough Athletic vs Thameside Amateurs	1-2
Haywards Heath vs Poole Town	1-2
Hitchin Town vs Romford	2-4
Ilford vs Hendon	1-5
Leytonstone vs Vauxhall Motors	4-2

Lowestoft Town vs Boldmere St. Michael's	1-2
Moor Green vs St. Albans City	3-1
Oxford City vs Redhill	3-2
Pegasus vs Smethwick Highfield	4-1
Ryde Sports vs Clevedon	2-4
Salts (Saltaire) vs Willington	3-5
Sheffield vs Yorkshire Amateurs	1-2
Shildon vs Bishop Auckland	3-2
South Bank vs Norton Woodseats	1-2
Stanley United vs Crook Colliery Welfare	1-4
Tilbury vs Gorleston	2-0
Tooting & Mitcham United vs Metropolitan Police	0-2
Walton & Hersham vs Dulwich Hamlet	1-0
Wealdstone vs Walthamstow Avenue	2-0
Wimbledon vs Salisbury	2-1
Woking vs Kingstonian	3-1
Wycombe Wanderers vs Barking	5-5
Yiewsley vs Sutton United	0-4
Marine (Crosby) received a bye	

First Round Replays

Barking vs Wycombe Wanderers	2-0
Briggs Sports vs Edgware Town	2-1*

* following a protest by Briggs Sports

Second Round

Bromley vs Wimbledon	6-1
Clevedon vs Billingham Synthonia	2-4
Erith & Belvedere vs Woking	4-0
Finchley vs Barking	2-3
Marine (Crosby) vs Tilbury	3-1
Moor Green vs Ferryhill Athletic	3-1
Oxford City vs Leytonstone	1-6
Pegasus vs Brentwood & Warley	2-1
Poole Town vs Hendon	0-1
Romford vs Brigg Sports	1-0
Shildon vs Thameside Amateurs	0-2
Sutton United vs Boldmere St. Michael's	1-0
Walton & Hersham vs Norton Woodseats	3-0
Wealdstone vs Metropolitan Police	1-1
Willington vs Cambridge Town	3-0
Yorkshire Amateurs vs Crook Colliery Welfare	1-1

Second Round Replays

Crook Colliery Welfare vs Yorkshire Amateurs	4-2
Metropolitan Police vs Wealdstone	1-3

Third Round

Barking vs Bromley	1-5
Billingham Synthonia vs Hendon	2-1
Crook Colliery Welfare vs Erith & Belvedere	2-2
Leytonstone vs Sutton United	7-0
Marine (Crosby) vs Walton & Hersham	4-1

49

Pegasus vs Willington	3-2
Romford vs Moor Green	5-1
Wealdstone vs Thameside Amateurs	2-0

Third Round Replay

Erith & Belvedere vs Crook Colliery Welfare	0-2

Fourth Round

Billingham Synthonia vs Romford	1-2
Crook Colliery Welfare vs Marine (Crosby)	3-2
Leytonstone vs Wealdstone	0-0
Pegasus vs Bromley	3-4

Fourth Round Replay

Wealdstone vs Leytonstone	0-4

Semi-Finals

Bromley vs Leytonstone	0-0
(at Highbury)	
Crook Colliery Welfare vs Romford	2-2
(at Sunderland)	

Semi-Final Replays

Leytonstone vs Bromley	0-2
(at Stamford Bridge)	
Romford vs Crook Colliery Welfare	3-0
(at Upton Park)	

Final

Bromley vs Romford	1-0
(at Wembley Stadium 23 April 1949)	

Attendance: 93,000

Bromley: Cornthwaite, Cameron, Yenson, T. Fuller, C. Fuller, Fright, Martin, Hopper, Brown, Dunmall, Ruddy
Scorer: Hopper
Romford: Ivey, Collier, Fryatt, Mackenzie, Barton, Regan, Brooks, Maddick, Bridge, Jennings, Patterson
Referee: P. Stevens (Bedfordshire)

1949-50 Amateur Cup

First Round

Barking vs Brentwood & Warley	6-4
Barnet vs Woking	3-1
Billingham Synthonia vs Crook Town	2-3
Bromley vs Thameside Amateurs	11-2
Bungay Town vs Wycombe Wanderers	0-4
Cambridge Town vs Vauxhall Motors	1-1
Cheshunt Sports vs Ryde Sports	2-1
Clapton vs Haywards Heath	5-0

Dulwich Hamlet vs Oxford City	2-1
Erith & Belvedere vs Pegasus	1-1
Grays Athletic vs Finchley	1-2
Hendon vs Bowater Lloyds	3-0
Hitchin Town vs Hayes	1-3
Hounslow Town vs Tooting & Mitcham United	3-2
Ilford vs Tilbury	0-0
Jack Mould's Athletic vs Evenwood Town	2-3
Kingstonian vs Wimbledon	0-2
Leytonstone vs Bristol St. George	2-0
Marine vs Boldmere St. Michael's	2-0
Moor Green vs Smethwick Highfield	1-0
Norton Woodseats vs Ferryhill Athletic	2-4
Penrith vs Willington	0-2
Redhill vs Bournemouth Gasworks Athletic	0-1
Romford vs Windsor & Eton	3-2
Salisbury vs Wealdstone	4-1
Sheffield vs Yorkshire Amateurs	3-2
South Bank vs Bishop Auckland	0-2
St. Albans City vs Walton & Hersham	4-2
Sutton United vs Wolverton Town & B.R.	1-1
Tow Law Town vs Stork	2-2
Walthamstow Avenue vs Metropolitan Police	4-3
Whitby Town vs Shildon	2-3

First Round Replays

Pegasus vs Erith & Belvedere	5-2
Stork vs Tow Law Town	2-1
Tilbury vs Ilford	1-2
Vauxhall Motors vs Cambridge Town	0-4
Wolverton Town & B.R. vs Sutton United	1-2

Second Round

Barking vs Barnet	3-1
Bishop Auckland vs Ilford	3-2
Bournemouth Gasworks Athletic vs Cambridge Town	0-2
Cheshunt Sports vs Bromley	2-1
Evenwood Town vs Moor Green	0-2
Finchley vs Hendon	1-0
Hayes vs Leytonstone	1-3
Marine vs Shildon	2-0
Romford vs Clapton	0-1
St. Albans City vs Stork	1-0
Salisbury vs Dulwich Hamlet	0-2
Sheffield vs Wimbledon	2-3
Sutton United vs Hounslow Town	0-1
Walthamstow Avenue vs Pegasus	3-1
Willington vs Ferryhill Athletic	3-1
Wycombe Wanderers vs Crook Town	1-0

Third Round

Bishop Auckland vs Moor Green	3-1
Cambridge Town vs Leytonstone	1-3
Clapton vs Barking	1-2

Finchley vs Marine	3-1
Hounslow Town vs Walthamstow Avenue	3-1
St. Albans City vs Cheshunt Sports	5-2
Willington vs Wimbledon	4-2
Wycombe Wanderers vs Dulwich Hamlet	3-1

Fourth Round

Barking vs Hounslow Town	5-2
Finchley vs Bishop Auckland	1-3
Leytonstone vs Willington	2-3
Wycombe Wanderers vs St. Albans City	4-1

Semi-Finals

Willington vs Barking	2-1
(at Middlesbrough)	
Wycombe Wanderers vs Bishop Auckland	1-2
(at Brentford)	

Final

| Bishop Auckland vs Willington | 0-4 |
| (at Wembley Stadium 22 April 1950) | |

Attendance: 88,000

Willington: Snowdon, Craggs, Howe, Leuthwaite, Yeardley, Dodd, Robinson, Taylor, Larmouth, Armstrong, Rutherford
Scorers: Taylor, Rutherford, Larmouth, Armstrong
Bishop Auckland: Washington, Coxon, Farrer, Taylor, Davison, Nimmins, Major, Hardisty, McIlvenny, Gilholme, Palmer
Referee: A. Murdoch (Sheffield & Hallamshire)

1950-51 Amateur Cup

First Round

Barnet vs Worthing	4-1
Billingham Synthonia vs Norton Woodseats	2-1
Boldmere St. Michael's vs Hayes	0-0
Brentwood & Warley vs Westbury United	1-1
Bromley vs Dulwich Hamlet	5-0
Bungay Town vs Histon Institute	4-3
Cambridge Town vs Clapton	3-2
Cheshunt vs Dagenham	1-4
Crook Town vs Yorkshire Amateurs	2-0
Eastbourne vs Barking	1-0
Edgware Town vs Kingstonian	2-2
Evenwood Town vs Bishop Auckland	0-2
Gosport Borough Athletic vs Pegasus	3-4
Hallam vs Whitby Town	1-2
Harwich & Parkeston vs Hounslow Town	1-5
Hendon vs Smethwick Highfield	2-0
Hitchin Town vs St. Albans City	1-0

Ilford vs Briggs Sports	1-0
Jack Mould's Athletic vs Woking	2-3
Leytonstone vs Wealdstone	3-2
Metropolitan Police vs Saltash United	4-2
Moor Green vs Romford	2-2
Oxford City vs Erith & Belvedere	4-2
Rawmarsh Welfare vs Ferryhill Athletic	2-2
Sheffield vs Penrith	4-1
Shildon vs Bearpark Colliery Welfare	2-1
Slough Town vs Poole Town	4-1
Tooting & Mitcham United vs Letchworth Town	7-1
Walton & Hersham vs Salisbury	0-0
Willington vs Marine (Liverpool)	1-0
Wimbledon vs Sheppey United	2-0
Wycombe Wanderers vs Walthamstow Avenue	2-2

First Round Replays

Ferryhill Athletic vs Rawmarsh Welfare	2-1
Hayes vs Boldmere St. Michael's	5-0
Kingstonian vs Edgware Town	2-1
Romford vs Moor Green	0-2
Salisbury vs Walton & Hersham	1-3
Walthamstow Avenue vs Wycombe Wanderers	3-0
Westbury United vs Brentwood & Warley	1-3

Second Round

Billingham Synthonia vs Bromley	1-3
Bishop Auckland vs Shildon	3-1
Brentwood & Warley vs Ferryhill Athletic	5-1
Bungay Town vs Hendon	0-3
Crook Town vs Hounslow Town	4-2
Dagenham vs Walthamstow Avenue	0-0
Eastbourne vs Sheffield	2-2
Hitchin Town vs Barnet	2-2
Ilford vs Walton & Hersham	1-3
Leytonstone vs Hayes	1-4
Oxford City vs Metropolitan Police	4-2
Slough Town vs Pegasus	1-3
Tooting & Mitcham United vs Kingstonian	4-2
Whitby Town vs Cambridge Town	1-1
Willington vs Moor Green	3-1
Woking vs Wimbledon	1-1

Second Round Replays

Barnet vs Hitchin Town	3-0
Cambridge Town vs Whitby Town	0-1
Sheffield vs Eastbourne	0-2
Walthamstow Avenue vs Dagenham	3-1
Wimbledon vs Woking	3-2

Third Round

| Barnet vs Eastbourne | 6-1 |
| Bishop Auckland vs Whitby Town | 7-2 |

Brentwood & Warley vs Pegasus	2-3
Hayes vs Bromley	0-2
Hendon vs Walthamstow Avenue	0-0
Oxford City vs Crook Town	2-2
Tooting & Mitcham United vs Wimbledon	2-2
Willington vs Walton & Hersham	0-1

Third Round Replays

Crook Town vs Oxford City	0-2
Walthamstow Avenue vs Hendon	0-2
Wimbledon vs Tooting & Mitcham United	2-2

Third Round Second Replay

Tooting & Mitcham United vs Wimbledon	1-1
(at Tooting)	

Third Round Third Replay

Wimbledon vs Tooting & Mitcham United	3-1
(at Wimbledon)	

Fourth Round

Barnet vs Bromley	0-2
Bishop Auckland vs Walton & Hersham	2-1
Oxford City vs Pegasus	0-3
Wimbledon vs Hendon	1-1

Fourth Round Replay

Hendon vs Wimbledon	2-0

Semi-Finals

Bishop Auckland vs Bromley	3-2
(at Leeds)	
Pegasus vs Hendon	1-1
(at Highbury)	

Semi-Final Replay

Hendon vs Pegasus	2-3
(at Crystal Palace)	

Final

Pegasus vs Bishop Auckland	2-1
(at Wembley Stadium 21 April 1951)	

Attendance: 100,000

Pegasus: Brown, Cowen, Maughan, Platt, Shearwood, Saunders, Pawson, Dutchman, Tanner, Carr, Potts
Scorers: Potts, Tanner
Bishop Auckland: White, Marshall, Farrer, Hardisty, Davison, Nimmins, Taylor, Anderson, McIlvenny, Williamson, Edwards
Scorer: Nimmins
Referee: A.E. Ellis (W. Riding)

1951-52 Amateur Cup

First Round

Barking vs Hayes	4-0
Billingham Synthonia vs Evenwood Town	3-3
Brentwood & Warley vs Salisbury	2-1
Briggs Sports vs Sheppey United	6-2
Cambridge City vs Leyton	1-2
Cheshunt vs Wycombe Wanderers	1-6
Corinthian Casuals vs Sutton United	2-1
Eastbourne vs Smethwick Highfield	3-0
Erith & Belvedere vs Tooting & Mitcham United	1-1
Histon Institute vs Boldmere St. Michael's	1-2
Hitchin Town vs Ilford	2-2
Kingstonian vs Pegasus	0-4
Letchworth Town vs Bromley	0-5
Moor Green vs Dulwich Hamlet	0-1
Norton Woodseats vs Wolsingham Welfare	1-2
Rawmarsh Welfare vs Bishop Auckland	1-5
Redhill vs Harwich & Parkeston	5-1
St. Albans City vs Barnet	0-1
Saltash United vs Oxford City	1-4
Salts vs Crook Town	3-4
Sheffield vs Shildon	4-2
Slough Town vs Hendon	2-3
Southall vs Leytonstone	4-1
Stowmarket Town vs Romford	0-2
Tilbury vs Frome Town	1-1
Walsall Wood vs Walton & Hersham	2-3
Willington vs Marine	2-4
Walthamstow Avenue vs Hounslow Town	2-0
Whitby Town vs South Bank	2-2
Wimbledon vs Clapton	2-1
Woking vs Keynsham Town	3-2
Yorkshire Amateurs vs Ferryhill Athletic	5-3

First Round Replays

Evenwood Town vs Billingham Synthonia	1-1*
Frome Town vs Tilbury	1-1
Ilford vs Hitchin Town	3-3*
South Bank vs Whitby Town	1-5
Tooting & Mitcham United vs Erith & Belvedere	0-1
* abandoned during extra time	

First Round Second Replays

Billingham Synthonia vs Evenwood Town	2-6
(at Shildon)	
Frome Town vs Tilbury	2-5
(at Enfield)	
Ilford vs Hitchin Town	3-1
(at Wealdstone)	

Second Round

Barking vs Corinthian Casuals	0-1

Barnet vs Whitby Town	1-0
Boldmere St. Michael's vs Romford	3-3
Brentwood & Warley vs Eastbourne	3-1
Bromley vs Yorkshire Amateurs	2-0
Crook Town vs Pegasus	1-1
Evenwood Town vs Dulwich Hamlet	1-2
Hendon vs Bishop Auckland	2-2
Ilford vs Wimbledon	1-2
Oxford City vs Leyton	0-1
Redhill vs Walton & Hersham	0-1
Southall vs Walthamstow Avenue	2-4
Tilbury vs Sheffield	1-0
Woking vs Marine	0-3
Wolsingham Welfare vs Briggs Sports	0-0
Wycombe Wanderers vs Erith & Belvedere	1-0

Second Round Replays

Bishop Auckland vs Hendon	5-1
Briggs Sports vs Wolsingham Welfare	4-0
Pegasus vs Crook Town	0-1
Romford vs Boldmere St. Michael's	4-0

Third Round

Barnet vs Bromley	4-2
Bishop Auckland vs Walton & Hersham	1-3
Briggs Sports vs Brentwood & Warley	4-0
Corinthian Casuals vs Wimbledon	0-3
Crook Town vs Romford	4-4
Leyton vs Dulwich Hamlet	4-2
Tilbury vs Walthamstow Avenue	0-2
Wycombe Wanderers vs Marine	1-0

Third Round Replay

Romford vs Crook Town	1-3

Fourth Round

Barnet vs Wycombe Wanderers	2-0
Crook Town vs Walton & Hersham	0-0
Leyton vs Briggs Sports	3-1
Wimbledon vs Walthamstow Avenue	0-0

Fourth Round Replays

Walthamstow Avenue vs Wimbledon	1-1
Walton & Hersham vs Crook Town	2-0

Fourth Round Second Replay

Wimbledon vs Walthamstow Avenue	0-3
(at Highbury)	

Semi-Finals

Barnet vs Leyton	1-2
(at Tottenham)	

Walton & Hersham vs Walthamstow Avenue	0-3
(at Fulham)	

Final

Walthamstow Avenue vs Leyton	2-1
(at Wembley Stadium 26 April 1952)	

Attendance: 100,000

Walthamstow Avenue: Gerula, Young, Stratton, Lucas, Brahan, Saunders, Rossiter, Bailey, Lewis, Hall, Camis
Scorers: Lewis, Hall
Leyton: Sullivan, Dixon, Pullinger, Gardiner, Yenson, Casey, Fitch, Facey, McIntree, Goddard, Skipp
Scorer: Skipp
Referee: J.V. Sherlock (Sheffield)

1952-53 Amateur Cup

First Round

Barking vs Kingstonian	3-1
Brentwood & Warley vs Corinthian Casuals	0-5
Cambridge City vs Anstey Nomads	2-1
Carshalton Athletic vs Ilford	1-0
Clevedon vs Briggs Sports	4-0
Cockfield vs Sheffield	3-2
Dulwich Hamlet vs Ware	3-2
Eastbourne vs Slough Town	1-4
Ferryhill Athletic vs I.C.I. Alkali	1-2
Finchley vs Erith & Belvedere	2-0
Harrogate vs Billingham Synthonia	2-1
Hayes vs Pegasus	2-4
Hendon vs Boldmere St. Michael's	4-0
Histon vs Dartmouth United	3-3
Hitchin Town vs Wycombe Wanderers	0-0
Leyton vs Bromley	1-2
Leytonstone vs Frome Town	6-1
Marine vs Crook Town	1-0
Redhill vs Hallam	2-2
St. Albans City vs Romford	4-4
Saltash United vs Southall	2-2
Salts vs Willington	0-3
Shildon vs Bishop Auckland	2-7
Sutton United vs Hounslow Town	3-5
Tooting & Mitcham United vs Oxford City	5-0
Walton & Hersham vs Tilbury	1-0
Wealdstone vs Moor Green	1-1
Whitby Town vs Evenwood Town	2-3
Whitton vs Harwich & Parkeston	1-1
Wimbledon vs Walthamstow Avenue	1-3
Woking vs Barnet	3-3
Yorkshire Amateurs vs Whitley Bay	0-0

53

First Round Replays

Barnet vs Woking	2-0
Dartmouth United vs Histon	3-2
Hallam vs Redhill	1-1
Harwich & Parkeston vs Whitton	4-2
Moor Green vs Wealdstone	1-3
Romford vs St. Albans City	4-0
Southall vs Saltash United	2-1
Whitley Bay vs Yorkshire Amateurs	0-2
Wycombe Wanderers vs Hitchin Town	2-0

First Round Second Replay

Redhill vs Hallam	0-2
(at Peterborough)	

1953 Amateur Cup Final

B. King, goalkeeper for Harwich & Parkeston, faces heavy odds when clearing from a Pegasus corner.
The 6-0 Pegasus win was watched by 100,000 spectators

Second Round

Carshalton Athletic vs Romford	2-3
Clevedon vs Dartmouth United	5-0
Corinthian Casuals vs Finchley	4-1
Hallam vs Dulwich Hamlet	1-0
(at Hillsborough)	
Harwich & Parkeston vs Harrogate	3-2
Hendon vs Hounslow Town	1-2
I.C.I. Alkali vs Leytonstone	2-3
Marine vs Evenwood Town	1-2
Pegasus vs Cockfield	5-0
Slough Town vs Barking	2-1
Southall vs Bishop Auckland	2-0
Tooting & Mitcham United vs Cambridge City	4-2
Walthamstow Avenue vs Wealdstone	0-0
Willington vs Bromley	2-1
Wycombe Wanderers vs Barnet	2-1
Yorkshire Amateurs vs Walton & Hersham	1-2

Second Round Replay

Wealdstone vs Walthamstow Avenue	1-0

Third Round

Clevedon vs Harwich & Parkeston	1-2
Corinthian Casuals vs Pegasus	0-1
Hounslow Town vs Tooting & Mitcham United	1-1
Leytonstone vs Hallam	3-1
Southall vs Wealdstone	3-0
Walton & Hersham vs Evenwood Town	3-1
Willington vs Slough Town	1-1
Wycombe Wanderers vs Romford	0-5

Third Round Replays

Slough Town vs Willington	3-2
Tooting & Mitcham United vs Hounslow Town	2-1

Fourth Round

Leytonstone vs Harwich & Parkeston	3-4
Slough Town vs Pegasus	0-2
Southall vs Romford	1-1
Tooting & Mitcham United vs Walton & Hersham	0-0

Fourth Round Replays

Romford vs Southall	1-2
Walton & Hersham vs Tooting & Mitcham United	0-0

Fourth Round Second Replay

Tooting & Mitcham United vs Walton & Hersham	1-2
(at Kingstonian)	

Semi-Finals

Southall vs Pegasus	1-1
(at Highbury)	
Walton & Hersham vs Harwich & Parkeston	1-3
(at Brentford)	

Semi-Final Replay

Southall vs Pegasus	1-2
(at Fulham)	

Final

Pegasus vs Harwich & Parkeston	6-0
(at Wembley Stadium 11 April 1953)	

Attendance: 100,000

Pegasus: Brown, Alexander, McKenna, Vowels, Shearwood, Saunders, Pawson, Carr, Laybourne, Lunn, Sutcliffe
Scorers: Saunders, Sutcliffe 2, Carr 2, Laybourne
Harwich & Parkeston: King, Nightingale, Tyrell, Christie, Bloss, Haugh, Stremp, Pearson, Davies, Cooper, Jennings
Referee: W.J. Edwards (Somerset)

1953-54 Amateur Cup

First Round

Banstead Athletic vs Leytonstone	3-4
Barnet vs Sutton United	7-0
Billingham Synthonia vs Salts	4-4
Brentwood & Warley vs Erith & Belvedere	1-6
Briggs Sports vs Bournemouth Gasworks Athletic	3-1
Cambridge City vs Barking	2-1
Cockfield vs Whitley Bay Athletic	2-0
Dagenham vs Bromley	1-2
Dartmouth United vs St. Albans City	1-3
Dulwich Hamlet vs Slough Town	3-1
Evenwood Town vs Hallam	0-1
Ferryhill Athletic vs Marine	2-1
Finchley vs Harwich & Parkeston	3-0
Gedling Colliery vs Yorkshire Amateurs	1-0
Harrogate & District Railway vs Northern Nomads	2-2
Hayes vs Carshalton Athletic	1-0
Hitchin Town vs Crittall's Athletic	4-0
Hounslow Town vs Moor Green	5-1
I.C.I. Alkali vs Bishop Auckland	0-6
Leyton vs Sheppey United	1-1
Pegasus vs Clevedon	3-0
Romford vs Thetford Town	3-0
Sheffield vs Willington	0-2
Shildon vs Crook Town	0-3
Southall vs Corinthian Casuals	0-2

Stevenage Town vs Wimbledon   1-3
Walthamstow Avenue vs Smethwick Town   2-1
Walton & Hersham vs Ilford   3-0
Ware vs Nanpean Rovers   6-2
Wealdstone vs Hendon   3-3
Woking vs Kingstonian   4-1
Wycombe Wanderers vs Tooting & Mitcham United   5-0

First Round Replays

Hendon vs Wealdstone   3-1
Northern Nomads vs Harrogate & District Railway   5-2
Salts vs Billingham Synthonia   5-2
Sheppey United vs Leyton   3-2

Second Round

Bishop Auckland vs Ware   6-1
Bromley vs Cockfield   2-1
Corinthian Casuals vs Hallam   0-1
Dulwich Hamlet vs Barnet   1-1
Finchley vs Ferryhill Athletic   4-1
Gedling Colliery vs Pegasus   1-6
Hendon vs Hayes   4-2
Hitchin Town vs Erith & Belvedere   1-0
Northern Nomads vs Willington   3-3
Romford vs Crook Town   1-1
St. Albans City vs Briggs Sports   1-2
Salts vs Hounslow Town   1-2
Sheppey United vs Wimbledon   1-0
Walthamstow Avenue vs Cambridge City   5-0
Walton & Hersham vs Woking   3-1
Wycombe Wanderers vs Leytonstone   0-0

Second Round Replays

Barnet vs Dulwich Hamlet   2-1
Crook Town vs Romford   6-0
Willington vs Northern Nomads   3-1
Wycombe Wanderers vs Leytonstone   0-0

Second Round Second Replay

Leytonstone vs Wycombe Wanderers   1-2
(at Dulwich Hamlet)

Third Round

Barnet vs Hitchin Town   1-1
Bishop Auckland vs Hallam   5-0
Briggs Sports vs Bromley   1-0
Crook Town vs Walton & Hersham   5-0
Hendon vs Finchley   1-1
Hounslow Town vs Wycombe Wanderers   3-0
Pegasus vs Willington   1-1
Walthamstow Avenue vs Sheppey United   4-0

Third Round Replays

Finchley vs Hendon   2-1
Hitchin Town vs Barnet   3-1
Willington vs Pegasus   2-4

Fourth Round

Bishop Auckland vs Hounslow Town   4-2
Briggs Sports vs Pegasus   3-0
Crook Town vs Hitchin Town   10-1
Finchley vs Walthamstow Avenue   1-1

Fourth Round Replay

Walthamstow Avenue vs Finchley   1-0

Semi-Finals

Bishop Auckland vs Briggs Sports   5-1
(at Newcastle)
Walthamstow Avenue vs Crook Town   1-1
(at Tottenham)

Semi-Final Replay

Crook Town vs Walthamstow Avenue   3-2
(at Sunderland)

Final

Bishop Auckland vs Crook Town   2-2
(at Wembley Stadium 10 April 1954)
Attendance: 100,000

Crook Town: Jarrie, Riley, Steward, Jeffs, Davison, Taylor, Appleby, Thompson, Harrison, Williamson, McMillan
Scorers: Thompson, Appleby
Bishop Auckland: Sharratt, Marshall, Frye, Hardisty, Cresswell, Nimmins, Major, Dixon, Oliver, O'Connell, Watson
Scorers: Dixon, Oliver
Referee: A. Bond (Middlesex)

Final Replay

Crook Town vs Bishop Auckland   2-2
(at St. James' Park, Newcastle 19 April 1954)
Attendance: 56,008

Crook Town: Jarrie, Riley, Steward, Jeffs, Davison, Taylor, Appleby, Thompson, Harrison, Coxon, McMillan
Scorer: Harrison 2
Bishop Auckland: Sharratt, Marshall, Stewart, Hardisty, Cresswell, Wilkinson, Major, Dixon, Oliver, O'Connell, Watson
Scorer: Oliver 2
Referee: A. Bond (Middlesex)

Final Second Replay

Bishop Auckland vs Crook Town	0-1

(at Ayresome Park, Middlesbrough 22 April 1954)

Attendance: 36,727

Crook Town: Jarrie, Riley, Steward, Jeffs, Davison, Taylor, Appleby, Thompson, Harrison, Coxon, McMillan
Scorer: Harrison
Bishop Auckland: Sharratt, Marshall, Stewart, Hardisty, Cresswell, Wilkinson, Major, Dixon, Oliver, O'Connell, Watson
Referee: A. Bond (Middlesex)

1954-55 Amateur Cup

First Round

Alton Town vs Banstead Athletic	2-1
Barnet vs Hitchin Town	0-2
Bromley vs Bungay Town	4-0
Cambridge City vs Thetford Town	3-2
Carshalton Athletic vs Leytonstone	3-1
Cockfield vs Northern Nomads	1-2
Crook Town vs Willington	0-1
Dartmouth United vs Hendon	3-3
Dulwich Hamlet vs Walton & Hersham	0-0
Erith & Belvedere vs Harwich & Parkeston	2-0
Finchley vs Southall	4-3
Gedling Colliery vs Billingham Synthonia	3-3
Grays Athletic vs Anstey Nomads	1-3
Hallam vs Ferryhill Athletic	2-0
Ilford vs Briggs Sports	1-0
Kingstonian vs Aylesbury United	2-0
Leyton vs Hayes	2-3
Marine vs Shildon	0-1
Norton Woodseats vs Salts	4-2
Pegasus vs Dagenham	4-0
Redhill vs Hounslow Town	3-3
Sheppey United vs Saltash Town	2-0
Stevenage Town vs Corinthian Casuals	3-1
Stork vs Bishop Auckland	1-3
Tooting & Mitcham United vs Wimbledon	1-1
Uxbridge vs Romford	4-2
Walthamstow Avenue vs Moor Green	4-0
Ware vs Clevedon	3-2
West Auckland Town vs Sheffield	2-2
Woking vs St. Albans City	2-1
Wycombe Wanderers vs Wealdstone	1-1
Yorkshire Amateurs vs Evenwood Town	1-3

First Round Replays

Billingham Synthonia vs Gedling Colliery	4-0
Hendon vs Dartmouth United	2-1
Hounslow Town vs Redhill	6-0

Sheffield vs West Auckland Town	1-4
Walton & Hersham vs Dulwich Hamlet	3-1
Wealdstone vs Wycombe Wanderers	1-2
Wimbledon vs Tooting & Mitcham United	4-3

Second Round

Alton Town vs Uxbridge	3-1
Anstey Nomads vs Hayes	1-2
Billingham Synthonia vs Bromley	1-3
Bishop Auckland vs Erith & Belvedere	5-0
Finchley vs Sheppey United	0-0
Hallam vs West Auckland Town	1-2
Hendon vs Cambridge City	4-3
Hounslow Town vs Hitchin Town	3-3
Kingstonian vs Walton & Hersham	3-2
Northern Nomads vs Ilford	2-2
(at Ilford)	
Norton Woodseats vs Carshalton Athletic	1-4
Shildon vs Wimbledon	0-0
Stevenage Town vs Pegasus	2-5
Walthamstow Avenue vs Ware	11-0
Willington vs Evenwood Town	1-2
Wycombe Wanderers vs Woking	4-0

Second Round Replays

Hitchin Town vs Hounslow Town	1-2
Ilford vs Northern Nomads	2-1
Sheppey United vs Finchley	1-4
Wimbledon vs Shildon	2-1

Third Round

Alton Town vs Carshalton Athletic	1-1
Evenwood Town vs Finchley	2-3
Hayes vs Wimbledon	0-2
Hounslow Town vs Bromley	3-0
Kingstonian vs Bishop Auckland	3-12
Pegasus vs West Auckland Town	4-1
Walthamstow Avenue vs Hendon	0-1
Wycombe Wanderers vs Ilford	3-1

Third Round Replay

Carshalton Athletic vs Alton Town	4-3

Fourth Round

Bishop Auckland vs Finchley	1-1
Carshalton Athletic vs Hounslow Town	2-2
Wimbledon vs Hendon	1-1
Wycombe Wanderers vs Pegasus	0-0

Fourth Round Replays

Finchley vs Bishop Auckland	1-3
Hendon vs Wimbledon	4-1

Bishop Auckland F.C., winners of the 1955 Amateur Cup.

back row: J.R.E. Hardisty, T. Stewart (Captain), C. Cresswell, H. Sharratt, D. Marshall, J. Nimmins;
front row: J. Major, D.J. Lewin, R. Oliver, S. O'Connell, B. Edwards.

Hounslow Town vs Carshalton Athletic	6-1
Pegasus vs Wycombe Wanderers	1-2

Semi-Finals

Bishop Auckland vs Wycombe Wanderers (at Doncaster)	1-0
Hendon vs Hounslow Town (at Tottenham)	2-1

Final

Hendon vs Bishop Auckland (at Wembley Stadium 16 April 1955)	0-2

Attendance: 100,000

Bishop Auckland: Sharratt, Marshall, Stewart, Hardisty, Cresswell, Nimmins, Major, Lewin, Oliver, O'Connell, Edwards
Scorer: Lewin 2
Hendon: Ivey, Fisher, Beardsley, Topp, Adams, Austin, Saffery, Hvidsten, Bahler, Cunningham, Parker
Referee: R. Mann (Worcestershire)

1955-56 Amateur Cup

First Round

Bishop Auckland vs Crook Town	1-1
Briggs Sports vs Romford	2-0
Cambridge City vs Thetford Town	2-2
Clevedon United vs Carshalton Athletic	2-2
Corinthian Casuals vs Sheppey United	4-1
Dulwich Hamlet vs Harwich & Parkeston	3-1
Durham City vs Newton	5-1
Eastwood Town vs Shildon	0-1
Ely City vs Alton Town	0-3
Enfield vs Wimbledon	1-1
Hallam vs West Auckland Town	2-3
Hertford Town vs Eastbourne United	3-2
Hitchin Town vs Keynsham	8-1
Hounslow Town vs Ware	5-1
Ilford vs Erith & Belvedere	1-1
Kingstonian vs Bromley	3-1
Letchworth Town vs St. Albans City	1-1
Northern Nomads vs Gedling Colliery	2-2
Norton Woodseats vs Malvern Town	3-2

Pegasus vs Barnet	2-0
Penrith vs Billingham Synthonia	1-3
St. Austell vs Redhill	2-1
Salts vs Yorkshire Amateurs	2-1
Southall vs Uxbridge	2-0
Stork vs Ferryhill Athletic	2-2
Sutton United vs Clapton	1-1
Tooting & Mitcham United vs Hendon	2-1
Walthamstow Avenue vs Hayes	1-1
Walton & Hersham vs Finchley	2-7
Willington vs Evenwood Town	4-2
Woking vs Leytonstone	0-0
Wycombe Wanderers vs Dagenham	4-1

First Round Replays

Carshalton Athletic vs Clevedon United	3-1
Clapton vs Sutton United	3-2
Crook Town vs Bishop Auckland	3-4
Erith & Belvedere vs Ilford	3-1
Ferrhill Athletic vs Stork	1-0
Gedling Colliery vs Northern Nomads	4-2
Hayes vs Walthamstow Avenue	4-1
Leytonstone vs Woking	2-0
St. Albans City vs Letchworth Town	2-0
Thetford Town vs Cambridge City	1-3
Wimbledon vs Enfield	3-1

Second Round

Alton Town vs Southall	1-4
Briggs Sports vs Hitchin Town	0-2
Corinthian Casuals vs Wimbledon	3-2
Dulwich Hamlet vs Clapton	1-0
Durham City vs Norton Woodseats	1-2
Ferryhill Athletic vs Shildon	2-2
Gedling Colliery vs Bishop Auckland	1-4
Hayes vs Finchley	2-3
Hertford Town vs Kingstonian	0-3
Hounslow Town vs Erith & Belvedere	2-2
Pegasus vs Wycombe Wanderers	1-2
St. Albans City vs Cambridge City	4-1
St. Austell vs Carshalton Athletic	2-1
Salts vs Billingham Synthonia	3-2
Tooting & Mitcham United vs Leytonstone	2-0
West Auckland Town vs Willington	2-1

Second Round Replays

Erith & Belvedere vs Hounslow Town	1-2
Shildon vs Ferryhill Athletic	2-4

Third Round

Ferryhill Athletic vs Bishop Auckland	0-1
Finchley vs Hounslow Town	2-0
Hitchin Town vs Wycombe Wanderers	1-0
Kingstonian vs St. Austell	4-0
Norton Woodseats vs Dulwich Hamlet	2-5
St. Albans City vs Corinthian Casuals	0-1
Tooting & Mitcham United vs Southall	2-1
West Auckland Town vs Salts	5-1

Fourth Round

Corinthian Casuals vs Hitchin Town	3-3
Finchley vs Bishop Auckland	0-4
Kingstonian vs Tooting & Mitcham United	3-0
West Auckland Town vs Dulwich Hamlet	0-0

Fourth Round Replays

Dulwich Hamlet vs West Auckland Town	3-0
Hitchin Town vs Corinthian Casuals	0-5

Semi-Finals

Bishop Auckland vs Kingstonian	5-1
(at Newcastle)	
Dulwich Hamlet vs Corinthian Casuals	1-3
(at Stamford Bridge)	

Final

Corinthian Casuals vs Bishop Auckland	1-1
(at Wembley Stadium 7 April 1956)	

Attendance: 80,000

Bishop Auckland: Sharratt, Fryer, Stewart, Hardisty, Cresswell, Nimmins, McKenna, Lewin, Oliver, O'Connell, Edwards
Scorer: McKenna
Corinthian Casuals: Ahm, Alexander, Newton, Shuttleworth, Cowan, Vowels, Insole, Sanders, Laybourne, Citron, Kerruish
Scorer: Kerruish
Referee: J.M. Clough (Lancashire)

Final Replay

Bishop Auckland vs Corinthian Casuals	4-1
(at Ayresome Park, Middlesbrough 14 April 1956)	

Attendance: 30,000

Bishop Auckland: Sharratt, Marshall, Stewart, Hardisty, Cresswell, O'Connell, McKenna, Lewin, Oliver, Bradley, Edwards
Scorers: Lewin 2, Hardisty, Stewart
Corinthian Casuals: Ahm, Alexander, Newton, Shuttleworth, Cowan, Vowels, Insole, Sanders, Laybourne, Citron, Kerruish
Scorer: Citron
Referee: J.M. Clough (Lancashire)

1956-57 Amateur Cup

First Round

Alton Town vs Carshalton Athletic	4-1
Bishop Auckland vs Norton Woodseats	1-0
Bromley vs Tooting & Mitcham United	2-2
Cambridge City vs Dulwich Hamlet	1-1
Clapton vs Leyton	0-0
Clevedon vs Wimbledon	1-1
Eastwood Town vs Salts	2-4
Ely City vs Erith & Belvedere	2-2
Enfield vs Yiewsley	0-1
Gedling Colliery vs Hallam	1-0
Harwich & Parkeston vs Briggs Sports	1-4
Hayes vs Holt United	5-0
Hertford Town vs Corinthian Casuals	1-2
Hitchin Town vs Redhill	2-1
Hounslow Town vs Leytonstone	2-1
Malvern Town vs Billingham Synthonia	1-5
Newton vs Ferryhill Athletic	2-3
Pegasus vs Romford	1-2
St. Albans City vs Wycombe Wanderers	1-4
St. Austell vs Eastbourne United	0-2
Saltash United vs Kingstonian	2-4
Sheppey United vs Hemel Hempstead Town	3-0
Shildon vs Willington	2-3
Stockton vs Crook Town	0-3
Stork vs Evenwood Town	0-1
Sutton United vs Finchley	1-0
Walthamstow Avenue vs Woking	1-1
Walton & Hersham vs Ilford	1-4
Ware vs Hendon	1-1
West Auckland Town vs Durham City	2-0
Whitley Bay Athletic vs Yorkshire Amateurs	3-0
Winchester City vs Southall	2-1

First Round Replays

Dulwich Hamlet vs Cambridge City	3-0
Erith & Belvedere vs Ely City	7-3
Hendon vs Ware	4-0
Leyton vs Clapton	1-2
Tooting & Mitcham United vs Bromley	4-3
Wimbledon vs Clevedon	4-3
Woking vs Walthamstow Avenue	2-3

Second Round

Alton Town vs Hounslow Town	1-2
Billingham Synthonia vs West Auckland Town	1-1
Bishop Auckland vs Gedling Colliery	5-1
Briggs Sports vs Hendon	4-3
Corinthian Casuals vs Eastbourne United	2-2
Erith & Belvedere vs Sutton United	1-2
Evenwood Town vs Whitley Bay Athletic	2-1
Hitchin Town vs Dulwich Hamlet	1-5
Ilford vs Wimbledon	4-2
Salts vs Ferryhill Athletic	0-1
Tooting & Mitcham United vs Sheppey United	2-0
Walthamstow Avenue vs Romford	2-2
Willington vs Crook Town	1-2
Winchester City vs Hayes	1-2
Wycombe Wanderers vs Clapton	4-2
Yiewsley vs Kingstonian	0-1

Second Round Replays

Eastbourne United vs Corinthian Casuals	0-2
Romford vs Walthamstow Avenue	0-4
West Auckland Town vs Billingham Synthonia	3-2

Third Round

Briggs Sports vs Bishop Auckland	0-1
Crook Town vs Evenwood Town	1-1
Hayes vs Ferryhill Athletic	1-1
Ilford vs Walthamstow Avenue	4-0
Kingstonian vs Dulwich Hamlet	5-1
Tooting & Mitcham United vs Sutton United	1-1
West Auckland Town vs Corinthian Casuals	0-2
Wycombe Wanderers vs Hounslow Town	3-1

Third Round Replays

Evenwood Town vs Crook Town	1-2
Ferryhill Athletic vs Hayes	3-4
Sutton United vs Tooting & Mitcham United	0-3

Fourth Round

Crook Town vs Bishop Auckland	2-2
Ilford vs Wycombe Wanderers	3-3
Kingstonian vs Hayes	1-1
Tooting & Mitcham United vs Corinthian Casuals	1-3

Fourth Round Replays

Bishop Auckland vs Crook Town	2-0
Hayes vs Kingstonian	1-0
Wycombe Wanderers vs Ilford	2-0

Semi-Finals

Bishop Auckland vs Hayes (at Newcastle)	2-0
Corinthian Casuals vs Wycombe Wanderers (at Highbury)	2-4

Final

Wycombe Wanderers vs Bishop Auckland   1-3
(at Wembley Stadium 13 April 1957)

Attendance: 90,000

Bishop Auckland: Sharratt, Marshall, Childs, Thursby, Cresswell, Nimmins, Bradley, Lewin, Russell, Hardisty, Edwards
Scorers: Russell, Lewin, Bradley
Wycombe Wanderers: Syrett, Lawson, Westley, G. Truett, Wicks, J. Truett, Worley, Trott, Bates, Tomlin, Smith
Scorer: Smith
Referee: J.W. Topliss (Lincs.)

1957-58 Amateur Cup

First Round

Alton Town vs Walton & Hersham	3-1
Billingham Synthonia vs Eastwood Town	3-0
Bromley vs Cambridge City	2-0
Bungay Town vs Kingstonian	6-5
Clapton vs Southall	2-1
Devizes Town vs St. Albans City	3-1
Erith & Belvedere vs Romford	3-1
Durham City vs Methley United	6-0
Evenwood Town vs Ferryhill Athletic	1-1
Finchley vs Eastbourne United	2-1
Gedling Colliery vs Willington	0-2
Hendon vs Dulwich Hamlet	5-1
Hitchin Town vs Corinthian Casuals	0-1
Ilford vs Eastbourne	2-1
Maidstone United vs Dagenham	0-2
St. Austell vs Hayes	0-2
Saltash United vs Briggs Sports	1-2
Salts vs Stanley United	3-2
Sheppey United vs Barnet	1-3
Stockton vs Newton	4-0
Stork vs Bishop Auckland	1-1
Vauxhall Motors vs Hounslow Town	3-1
Walsall Wood vs West Auckland Town	0-3
Walthamstow Avenue vs Pegasus	2-2
Whitley Bay Athletic vs Crook Town	2-4
Wimbledon vs Tooting & Mitcham United	0-5
Winchester City vs Enfield	1-0
Woking vs Aveley	6-1
Wokingham Town vs Histon	4-0
Wycombe Wanderers vs Leytonstone	2-0
Yiewsley vs Sutton United	3-1
Yorkshire Amateurs vs Norton Woodseats	1-3

First Round Replays

Bishop Auckland vs Stork	3-2
Ferryhill Athletic vs Evenwood Town	2-1

Pegasus vs Walthamstow Avenue	3-1

Second Round

Barnet vs Yiewsley	6-0
Billingham Synthonia vs Willington	1-2
Bishop Auckland vs Tooting & Mitcham United	2-0
Bungay Town vs Ilford	0-4
Clapton vs Bromley	1-2
Corinthian Casuals vs Salts	10-0
Crook Town vs Briggs Sports	3-0
Dagenham vs Hayes	0-0
Devizes Town vs Vauxhall Motors	1-7
Finchley vs Alton Town	3-1
Hendon vs Woking	1-3
Norton Woodseats vs Wokingham Town	3-1
Pegasus vs Ferryhill Athletic	0-2
Stockton vs Durham City	0-0
West Auckland Town vs Erith & Belvedere	3-0
Wycombe Wanderers vs Winchester City	6-0

Second Round Replays

Durham City vs Stockton	3-4
Hayes vs Dagenham	3-0
Wokington Town vs Norton Woodseats	1-0

Third Round

Bromley vs Vauxhall Motors	1-3
Crook Town vs Corinthian Casuals	2-2
Ferryhill Athletic vs Barnet	3-3
Finchley vs Willington	3-0
Ilford vs Wycombe Wanderers	2-1
Stockton vs Bishop Auckland	2-1
Woking vs Hayes	5-1
Wokingham Town vs West Auckland Town	4-2†, 3-2

† a replay was ordered after Wokingham Town fielded an ineligible player

Third Round Replays

Barnet vs Ferryhill Athletic	4-2
Corinthian Casuals vs Crook Town	1-2

Fourth Round

Barnet vs Stockton	4-1
Crook Town vs Wokingham Town	3-2
Ilford vs Vauxhall Motors	3-0
Woking vs Finchley	3-2

Semi-Finals

Barnet vs Woking	1-1
(at Fulham)	
Crook Town vs Ilford	0-1
(at Sunderland)	

Final

Woking vs Ilford	3-0

(at Wembley Stadium 12 April 1958)

Attendance: 71,000

Woking: Burley, Ellerby, Parsons, Collingwood, Turner, Clacey, Littlejohn, Hebdon, Mortimore, Hamm, Stratton
Scorers: Hebdon 2, Stratton
Ilford: Gibbins, Simmons, Cross, Sharod, Whittall, Dodkins, Durston, Winch, Taylor, Butler, Castle
Referee: R.W. Clements (Birmingham)

1958-59 Amateur Cup

First Round

Alton Town vs Histon	2-1
Barnet vs Sheppey United	4-0
Billingham Synthonia vs Evenwood Town	0-4
Briggs Sports vs Maidstone United	0-0
Carshalton Athletic vs Wimbledon	2-0
Corinthian Casuals vs Harrow Town	1-1
Dulwich Hamlet vs Saltash United	4-0
Durham City vs Yorkshire Amateurs	0-2
Eastbourne United vs Harwich & Parkeston	0-0
Fareham Town vs Clapton	2-2
Ferryhill Athletic vs Crook Town	1-2
Finchley vs Bromley	0-2
Gedling Colliery vs Hallam	0-2
Hayes vs Dagenham	1-0
Hitchin Town vs Faversham Town	1-0
Hounslow Town vs Wycombe Wanderers	1-1*, 2-4
* match abandoned	
Norton Woodseats vs Whitby Town	2-5
Oxford City vs Ilford	3-1
Pegasus vs Kingstonian	1-0
Redhill vs Woking	6-3
Romford vs Leytonstone	0-1
Salts vs Loughborough Colleges	2-1
Southall vs Sutton United	0-0
Stockton vs Shildon	3-3
Stotford vs Erith & Belvedere	1-3
Vauxhall Motors vs Hendon	1-3
Walthamstow Avenue vs Devizes Town	3-1
Walton & Hersham vs Uxbridge	0-2
West Auckland Town vs I.C.I. Alkali	2-3
Whitley Bay vs Bishop Auckland	1-3
Willington vs Walsall Wood	1-0
Winchester City vs Tooting & Mitcham United	1-5

First Round Replays

Clapton vs Fareham Town	3-1
Harrow Town vs Corinthian Casuals	1-3
Harwich & Parkeston vs Eastbourne United	4-2

Maidstone United vs Briggs Sport	1-2
Shildon vs Stockton	2-0
Sutton United vs Southall	0-3

Second Round

Alton Town vs Hayes	3-1
Barnet vs Willington	8-4
Bishop Auckland vs Pegasus	0-0
Briggs Sports vs Whitby Town	2-1
Corinthian Casuals vs Hitchin Town	4-1
Erith & Belvedere vs Crook Town	2-5
Evenwood Town vs Hallam	2-2
Harwich & Parkeston vs Yorkshire Amateurs	0-0
Hendon vs Tooting & Mitcham United	2-0
I.C.I. Alkali vs Oxford City	3-7
Leytonstone vs Carshalton Athletic	2-0
Salts vs Uxbridge	3-1
Shildon vs Clapton	5-3
Southall vs Redhill	0-1
Walthamstow Avenue vs Bromley	4-0
Wycombe Wanderers vs Dulwich Hamlet	2-1

Second Round Replays

Hallam vs Evenwood Town	2-0*, 4-3
* match abandoned	
Pegasus vs Bishop Auckland	0-0
Yorkshire Amateurs vs Harwich & Parkeston	3-2

Second Round Second Replay

Bishop Auckland vs Pegasus	1-0

(at Hillsborough)

Third Round

Alton Town vs Leytonstone	0-3
Barnet vs Wycombe Wanderers	2-2
Bishop Auckland vs Redhill	3-2
Crook Town vs Oxford City	5-2
Hallam vs Hendon	0-1
Salts vs Briggs Sports	2-3
Shildon vs Corinthian Casuals	5-0
Walthamstow Avenue vs Yorkshire Amateurs	4-0

Third Round Replay

Wycombe Wanderers vs Barnet	0-1

Fourth Round

Barnet vs Bishop Auckland	2-1
Briggs Sports vs Crook Town	0-3
Leytonstone vs Hendon	3-3
Shildon vs Walthamstow Avenue	1-1

Fourth Round Replays

Hendon vs Leytonstone	1-2
Walthamstow Avenue vs Shildon	3-1

Semi-Finals

Barnet vs Walthamstow Avenue	0-0
(at Highbury)	
Crook Town vs Leytonstone	2-0
(at Sunderland)	

Semi-Final Replay

Walthamstow Avenue vs Barnet	0-2
(at Tottenham)	

Final

Barnet vs Crook Town	2-3
(at Wembley Stadium 18 April 1959)	

Attendance: 60,000

Crook Town: Snowball, Gardener, Steward, Carr, Bainbridge, Wilkie, Coates, O'Connell, Keating, Tracey, McMillan
Scorers: Tracey 2, Keating
Barnet: Goymer, Duncan, Cooper, Sleap, A. D'Arcy, Cantwell, Welch, D. D'Arcy, Brown, Harding, Drake
Scorer: Brown 2
Referee: A. Holland (Sheffield & Hallamshire)

1959-60 Amateur Cup

First Round

Alton Town vs Pegasus	1-2
Barnet vs Hayes	1-1
Beccles vs Enfield	1-6
Bromley vs Wealdstone	5-1
Clevedon vs Ilford	2-1
Corinthian Casuals vs Tooting & Mitcham United	2-2
Devizes Town vs Finchley	1-1
Ferryhill Athletic vs Sheffield	1-0
Ford United vs Woking	2-0
Hallam vs Willington	4-3
Hendon vs Vauxhall Motors	3-0
Histon vs Kingstonian	0-3
Hitchin Town vs Harwich & Parkeston	1-3
Hounslow Town vs Wycombe Wanderers	3-0
Letchworth Town vs Grays Athletic	2-1
Leytonstone vs Winchester City	3-0
Maidenhead United vs Sutton United	1-1
Maidstone United vs Erith & Belvedere	2-3
Marine vs Moor Green	3-1
Norton Woodseats vs Bishop Auckland	1-0
Redhill vs Leatherhead	1-1

Salts vs Whitby Town	1-0
Shildon vs Billingham Synthonia	4-4
Stanley United vs Loughborough Colleges	5-0
Stockton vs Evenwood Town	0-0
Uxbridge vs Clapton	4-1
Walthamstow Avenue vs Dagenham	2-1
Waterlooville vs Carshalton Athletic	0-1
West Auckland Town vs Doncaster United	1-0
Wimbledon vs Dulwich Hamlet	1-0
Worthing vs Southall	1-2
Yorkshire Amateurs vs Crook Town	0-3

First Round Replays

Billingham Synthonia vs Shildon	1-2
Evenwood Town vs Stockton	3-1
Finchley vs Devizes Town	4-0
Hayes vs Barnet	3-2
Leatherhead vs Redhill	0-1
Sutton United vs Maidenhead United	2-3
Tooting & Mitcham United vs Corinthian Casuals	3-1

Second Round

Bromley vs West Auckland Town	1-1
Carshalton Athletic vs Stanley United	3-1
Erith & Belvedere vs Shildon	2-7
Evenwood Town vs Walthamstow Avenue	2-2
Ferryhill Athletic vs Marine	1-0
Finchley vs Southall	1-1
Ford United vs Salts	4-0
Hallam vs Crook Town	2-6
Harwich & Parkeston vs Tooting & Mitcham United	1-3
Hayes vs Clevedon	6-2
Hendon vs Wimbledon	2-1
Hounslow Town vs Enfield	2-2
Kingstonian vs Letchworth Town	5-2
Leytonstone vs Redhill	1-2
Norton Woodseats vs Pegasus	4-1
Uxbridge vs Maidenhead United	1-4

Second Round Replays

Enfield vs Hounslow Town	3-2
Southall vs Finchley	2-2
Walthamstow Avenue vs Evenwood Town	2-0
West Auckland Town vs Bromley	3-0

Second Round Second Replay

Finchley vs Southall	3-3
(at Wealdstone)	

Second Round Third Replay

Southall vs Finchley	4-1
(at Southall)	

Third Round

Carshalton Athletic vs Norton Woodseats	3-0
Crook Town vs Walthamstow Avenue	1-0
Ford United vs Hayes	0-0
Kingstonian vs Ferryhill Athletic	3-3
Maidenhead United vs West Auckland Town	1-2
Redhill vs Hendon	0-6
Shildon vs Enfield	1-3
Tooting & Mitcham United vs Southall	1-1

Third Round Replays

Ferryhill Athletic vs Kingstonian	2-4
Hayes vs Ford United	5-3
Southall vs Tooting & Mitcham United	1-0

Fourth Round

Crook Town vs Hayes	2-1
Kingstonian vs Carshalton Athletic	4-0
Southall vs Enfield	0-1
West Auckland Town vs Hendon	1-1

Fourth Round Replay

Hendon vs West Auckland Town	2-0

Semi-Finals

Crook Town vs Kingstonian (at Newcastle)	1-2
Hendon vs Enfield (at Brentford)	2-0

Final

Hendon vs Kingstonian (at Wembley Stadium 23 April 1960)	2-1

Attendance: 60,000

Hendon: Shearing, Widdowfield, Harris, Topp, Fisher, Murphy, Candey, Figg, Spector, Quail, Howard
Scorers: Topp, Howard
Kingstonian: Groves, Davies, Bird, Richards, Ashworth, Gilson, K. Harris, Coates, Whing, Lindsay, Oakes
Scorer: Whing
Referee: J.W. Hunt (Hampshire)

1960-61 Amateur Cup

First Round

Bungay Town vs Leytonstone	0-0
Carshalton Athletic vs Hendon	2-2
Clapton vs Hayes	3-1
Corinthian Casuals vs Hertford Town	3-2
Crook Town vs Stanley United	1-1
Dulwich Hamlet vs Redhill	4-0
Erith & Belvedere vs Pegasus	3-3
Evenwood Town vs Ferryhill Athletic	1-2
Grays Athletic vs Finchley	2-3
Hallam vs Stratford Town	0-1*, 0-0
* match abandoned	
Harwich & Parkeston vs Barnet	3-2
Hitchin Town vs Ford United	4-0
Hounslow Town vs Fareham Town	2-0
Ilford vs Sutton United	2-5
Kingstonian vs Maidstone United	1-3
Loughborough Colleges vs Salts	6-1
Maidenhead United vs Alton Town	1-2
Norton Woodseats vs Eastwood Town	2-2
Shildon vs Billingham Synthonia	2-0
Southall vs Newbury Town	5-1
Stockton vs Penrith	0-3
Tooting & Mitcham United vs Bromley	2-3
Uxbridge vs Dagenham	0-0
Walthamstow Avenue vs Bishop's Stortford	3-0
Walton & Hersham vs Clevedon	10-0
Wealdstone vs Enfield	1-2
Westbury United vs Vauxhall Motors	0-0
Whitley Bay vs Harrogate & District Railway	4-2
Willington vs Bishop Auckland	1-1
Woking vs Chichester City	6-2
Wycombe Wanderers vs Wimbledon	1-2
Yorkshire Amateurs vs West Auckland Town	0-3

First Round Replays

Bishop Auckland vs Willington	3-1
Dagenham vs Uxbridge	1-2
Eastwood Town vs Norton Woodseats	2-3
Hendon vs Carshalton Athletic	2-1
Leytonstone vs Bungay Town	5-0
Pegasus vs Erith & Belvedere (at White City)	2-0
Stanley United vs Crook Town	2-0
Stratford Town vs Hallam	0-2
Vauxhall Motors vs Westbury United	1-4

Second Round

Alton Town vs Ferryhill Athletic	1-2
Bromley vs Pegasus	1-1
Corinthian Casuals vs Norton Woodseats	5-0
Enfield vs Maidstone United	0-2
Harwich & Parkeston vs Dulwich Hamlet	7-1
Hendon vs Walthamstow Avenue	0-2
Hitchin Town vs Southall	3-2
Leytonstone vs Uxbridge	3-0
Loughborough Colleges vs Bishop Auckland	3-1
Stanley United vs Penrith	1-1
Sutton United vs Finchley	1-1
Walton & Hersham vs Shildon	5-0

West Auckland Town vs Clapton	3-1
Westbury United vs Hallam	1-2
Whitley Bay vs Hounslow Town	3-1
Woking vs Wimbledon	1-5

Second Round Replays

Finchley vs Sutton United	0-2
Pegasus vs Bromley	1-2
Penrith vs Stanley United	3-2

Third Round

Harwich & Parkeston vs Walthamstow Avenue	2-7
Hitchin Town vs Ferryhill Athletic	3-2
Leytonstone vs Hallam	1-1
Loughborough Colleges vs Corinthian Casuals	2-1
Maidstone United vs Walton & Hersham	0-1
Penrith vs West Auckland Town	1-1
Sutton United vs Bromley	3-1
Wimbledon vs Whitley Bay	3-3

Third Round Replays

Hallam vs Leytonstone	0-3
West Auckland Town vs Penrith	2-2
Whitley Bay vs Wimbledon	2-2

Third Round Second Replays

| West Auckland Town vs Penrith (at Carlisle) | 1-0 |
| Wimbledon vs Whitley Bay (at Kingstonian) | 6-1 |

Fourth Round

Hitchin Town vs Loughborough Colleges	5-1
Leytonstone vs Sutton United	2-0
West Auckland Town vs Walton & Hersham	4-1
Wimbledon vs Walthamstow Avenue	0-1

Semi-Finals

| Walthamstow Avenue vs Hitchin Town (at White City) | 1-0 |
| West Auckland Town vs Leytonstone (at Sunderland) | 3-1 |

Final

| Walthamstow Avenue vs West Auckland Town (at Wembley Stadium 22 April 1961) | 2-1 |

Attendance: 45,000

Walthamstow Avenue: McGuire, Edwards, Bambridge, Andrews, Prince, Keenes, Groves, Minall, Lewis, Saggers, Harvey
Scorers: Groves, Lewis

West Auckland Town: Bowmaker, Siddle, Stafford, Mendum, Summerson, Carter, Briggs, Broomfield, Curtis, Skelton, Douglass
Scorer: Douglass
Referee: J.G. Williams (Notts)

1961-62 Amateur Cup

First Round

Barnet vs Sutton United	1-2
Bishop Auckland vs Whitby Town	2-0
Bishop's Stortford vs Gothic	3-0
Bromley vs Fareham Town	2-0
Carshalton Athletic vs Leytonstone	0-2
Clapton vs Hounslow Town	2-2
Corinthian Casuals vs Woking	2-3
Crook Town vs Ossett Albion	1-0
Dagenham vs Hitchin Town	6-2
Eastbourne vs Kingstonian	2-0
Eastwood Town vs Norton Woodseats	4-0
Evenwood Town vs Stanley United	1-3
Hallam vs Yorkshire Amateurs	1-2
Hemel Hempstead Town vs Tooting & Mitcham United	1-3
Ilford vs Wimbledon	0-1
Lydbrook Athletic vs Westbury United	2-1
Maidenhead United vs Wealdstone	3-1
Maidstone United vs Harwich & Parkeston	2-0
Pegasus vs Hendon	0-0
Penrith vs Billingham Synthonia	2-1
Redhill vs Enfield	0-2
St. Albans City vs Welton Rovers	6-0
Shildon vs Alvechurch	1-0
Uxbridge vs Finchley	1-1
Vauxhall Motors vs Dulwich Hamlet	0-2
Walthamstow Avenue vs Ford United	0-2
Walton & Hersham vs Hayes	1-0
West Auckland Town vs Northern Nomads	2-1
Whitley Bay vs Ferryhill Athletic	1-0
Willington vs Loughborough Colleges	1-2
Windsor & Eton vs Southall	1-1
Wycombe Wanderers vs Erith & Belvedere	2-1

First Round Replays

Finchley vs Uxbridge	1-0
Hendon vs Pegasus	6-1
Hounslow Town vs Clapton	3-0
Southall vs Windsor & Eton	0-1

Second Round

Bishop Auckland vs Lydbrook Athletic	5-0
Bishop's Stortford vs West Auckland Town	0-4
Bromley vs Yorkshire Amateurs	3-1

Crook Town vs Windsor & Eton	2-1
Eastbourne vs Woking	0-1
Eastwood Town vs Finchley	1-2
Hendon vs St. Albans City	0-3
(at Wealdstone)	
Hounslow Town vs Dulwich Hamlet	6-1
Loughborough Colleges vs Maidenhead United	4-0
Maidstone United vs Walton & Hersham	0-2
Penrith vs Leytonstone	0-0
Shildon vs Enfield	1-2
Stanley United vs Whitley Bay	2-1
Sutton United vs Wycombe Wanderers	1-4
Tooting & Mitcham United vs Dagenham	1-2
Wimbledon vs Ford United	6-0

Second Round Replay

| Leytonstone vs Penrith | 1-0 |

Third Round

Bishop Auckland vs Loughborough Colleges	2-0
Dagenham vs Crook Town	0-0
Enfield vs St. Albans City	0-0
Finchley vs Hounslow Town	0-0
Stanley United vs West Auckland Town	2-4
Walton & Hersham vs Bromley	2-3
Wimbledon vs Wycombe Wanderers	1-0
Woking vs Leytonstone	1-1

Third Round Replays

Crook Town vs Dagenham	2-1
Hounslow Town vs Finchley	2-0
Leytonstone vs Woking	1-0
St. Albans City vs Enfield	1-2

Fourth Round

Bromley vs Hounslow Town	1-1
Crook Town vs Wimbledon	2-0
Leytonstone vs Bishop Auckland	1-2
West Auckland Town vs Enfield	0-0

Fourth Round Replays

| Enfield vs West Auckland Town | 0-1 |
| Hounslow Town vs Bromley | 2-1 |

Semi-Finals

Crook Town vs West Auckland Town	2-0
(at Middlesbrough)	
Hounslow Town vs Bishop Auckland	2-1
(at Brentford)	

Final

| Hounslow Town vs Crook Town | 1-1 |

(at Wembley Stadium 14 April 1962)

Attendance: 43,000

Crook Town: Snowball, Gardener, Clarke, Storey, Heatherington, Brown, Sparks, Garbutt, Coates, Peary, McMillan

Scorer: McMillan

Hounslow Town: Rhodes, MacDonald, Creasey, Evans, Taylor, Digweed, Somers, Fennell, McHattie, Dipper, Patterson

Scorer: Patterson

Referee: J.K. Taylor (Wolverhampton)

Final Replay

| Crook Town vs Hounslow Town | 4-0 |

(at Ayresome Park, Middlesbrough 21 April 1962)

Attendance: 18,279

Crook Town: Snowball, Gardener, Clarke, Storey, Heatherington, Brown, Sparks, Garbutt, Coates, Peary, McMillan

Scorers: Coates 2, Sparks, McMillan

Hounslow Town: Rhodes, MacDonald, Creasey, Evans, Taylor, Digweed, Alder, Somers, McHattie, Dipper, Patterson

Referee: J.K. Taylor (Wolverhampton)

1962-63 Amateur Cup

First Round

Alton Town vs Eastbourne United	2-1
Barking vs Hendon	1-0
Barnet vs Cray Wanderers	3-0
(at Enfield)	
Bishop's Stortford vs Vauxhall Motors	1-0*, 5-0
* match abandoned	
Chesham United vs Corinthian Casuals	2-0
(at The Oval)	
Dagenham vs Leytonstone	1-2
Dulwich Hamlet vs Hitchin Town	1-2
Ferryhill Athletic vs Hallam	4-1
Finchley vs Enfield	0-6
Ford United vs Maidstone United	0-1
Harlow Town vs Letchworth Town	1-1
Harwich & Parkeston vs Walton & Hersham	3-3
Hounslow Town vs Kingstonian	1-3
Leatherhead vs Pinehurst	3-0
Loughborough Colleges vs Billingham Synthonia	3-0
Lydbrook Athletic vs Woking	0-1
(at Westbury)	
Maidenhead United vs Hayes	0-4
(at Hayes)	

Shildon vs Bishop Auckland	1-5
Stanley United vs Penrith	1-4
Stratford Town vs Guinness Exports	1-1
Sutton United vs Clapton	4-1
Tooting & Mitcham United vs St. Albans City	2-1
Tow Law Town vs Whitley Bay	0-0
(at Seaton Delaval)	
Walthamstow Avenue vs Grays Athletic	2-1
Welton Rovers vs Bromley	3-2
West Auckland Town vs Blackpool Rangers	2-3*
(at Evenwood) * match abandoned	
West Auckland Town vs Blackpool Rangers	5-1
(at Bishop Auckland)	
Whitby Town vs Crook Town	3-3
Willington vs Norton Woodseats	1-3
Wimbledon vs Southall	3-3
Windsor & Eton vs Eastbourne	0-3
Wycombe Wanderers vs Uxbridge	2-0
Yorkshire Amateurs vs Eastwood Town	2-1

First Round Replays

Crook Town vs Whitby Town	2-1
Guiness Exports vs Stratford Town	0-1
Letchworth Town vs Harlow Town	2-2
Southall vs Wimbledon	0-3
Walton & Hersham vs Harwich & Parkeston	1-0
Whitley Bay vs Tow Law Town	2-1
(at Billingham)	

First Round Second Replay

Harlow Town vs Letchworth Town	2-3
(at Letchworth)	

Second Round

Alton Town vs Letchworth Town	3-1
Barnet vs Kingstonian	2-0
Bishop Auckland vs West Auckland Town	1-3
Bishop's Stortford vs Norton Woodseats	6-2
Chesham United vs Wimbledon	1-3
Crook Town vs Walthamstow Avenue	0-0*, 3-0
* match abandoned	
Eastbourne vs Yorkshire Amateurs	1-1
Enfield vs Ferryhill Athletic	2-0
Leatherhead vs Hitchin Town	1-4
Leytonstone vs Loughborough Colleges	5-1
Maidstone United vs Sutton United	2-2
Stratford Town vs Penrith	2-1
Tooting & Mitcham United vs Welton Rovers	11-0
Whitley Bay vs Hayes	2-2
Woking vs Walton & Hersham	1-2
Wycombe Wanderers vs Barking	3-2

Second Round Replays

Hayes vs Whitley Bay	3-0
Sutton United vs Maidstone United	6-0
Yorkshire Amateurs vs Eastbourne	1-0

The 1963 Amateur Cup Final.

The second goal in Wimbledon's 4-2 victory over Sutton United scored by centre-forward Reynolds *(far right)*.
Sutton's Number 4, Shepherd, can be seen making a vain attempt to save the goal.

Third Round

Alton Town vs Crook Town	2-1
Barnet vs Wimbledon	0-1
Enfield vs Tooting & Mitcham United	3-2
Hayes vs Walton & Hersham	3-2
Hitchin Town vs Wycombe Wanderers	3-2
Leytonstone vs Yorkshire Amateurs	5-1
Sutton United vs Stratford Town	4-0
West Auckland Town vs Bishop's Stortford	0-0

Third Round Replay

Bishop's Stortford vs West Auckland Town	1-0

Fourth Round

Hitchin Town vs Hayes	2-2
Leytonstone vs Enfield	4-0
Sutton United vs Alton Town	1-0
Wimbledon vs Bishop's Stortford	1-0

Fourth Round Replay

Hayes vs Hitchin Town	0-1

Semi-Finals

Leytonstone vs Wimbledon	1-2
(at Highbury)	
Sutton United vs Hitchin Town	4-0
(at Fulham)	

Final

Wimbledon vs Sutton United	4-2
(at Wembley Stadium 4 May 1963)	

Attendance: 45,000

Wimbledon: Kelly, J. Martin, Willis, Ardrey, Law, Murphy, Brown, B. Martin, Reynolds, Hamm, Williams
Scorer: Reynolds 4
Sutton United: Roffey, Gamblin, Shears, Shepherd, Price, Clack, Bladon, Osborne, Bates, Hermitage, Goodall
Scorers: Goodall, Bladon
Referee: K. Dagnall (Lancashire)

1963-64 Amateur Cup

First Round

Alton Town vs Hayes	1-2
Alvechurch vs Penrith	1-1
Aveley vs Windsor & Eton	2-4
Berkhamsted Town vs Harrow Town	2-2
Bishop Auckland vs Whitley Bay	4-4
Bishop's Stortford vs Ford United	2-1
Bromley vs Corinthian Casuals	2-0
Clapton vs Hanham Athletic	1-0
Crook Town vs Stanley United	1-1
Dagenham vs Woking	0-0
Eastbourne vs Walthamstow Avenue	0-5
Enfield vs Finchley	2-1
Fareham Town vs Hendon	1-0
Ferryhill Athletic vs Norton Woodseats	3-0
Grays Athletic vs Southall	2-2
Harwich & Parkeston vs Leatherhead	4-2
Heys Old Boys vs West Auckland Town	2-2
Hitchin Town vs Tooting & Mitcham United	1-2
Hounslow vs Barnet	1-4
Kingstonian vs Stowmarket	1-0
Leytonstone vs Maidstone United	2-0
Loughborough Colleges vs Eastwood Town	1-6
Shildon vs Evenwood Town	2-3
Spennymoor United vs Stratford Town	3-0
Sutton United vs Oxford City	0-0
Uxbridge vs St. Albans City	2-6
Walton & Hersham vs Torpoint Athletic	5-4
Wealdstone vs Carshalton Athletic	1-1
Whitby Town vs Yorkshire Amateurs	7-0
Willington vs Guinness Exports	2-4
Wimbledon vs Maidenhead United	4-0
Wycombe Wanderers vs Dulwich Hamlet	3-0

First Round Replays

Carshalton Athletic vs Wealdstone	3-1
Harrow Town vs Berkhamsted Town	2-1
Oxford City vs Sutton United	1-2
Penrith vs Alvechurch	2-0
Southall vs Grays Athletic	0-2
Stanley United vs Crook Town	1-5
West Auckland Town vs Heys Old Boys	3-0
Whitley Bay vs Bishop Auckland	1-0
Woking vs Dagenham	3-1

Second Round

Bromley vs Sutton United	1-1
Clapton vs Barnet	0-1
Eastwood Town vs Woking	2-1
Ferryhill Athletic vs Bishop's Stortford	3-1
Guinness Exports vs Kingstonian	0-1
Harrow Town vs Carshalton Athletic	1-5
Harwich & Parkeston vs Evenwood Town	0-2
Hayes vs Crook Town	0-0
Penrith vs Grays Athletic	0-2
St. Albans City vs Whitby Town	0-2
Spennymoor United vs Leytonstone	2-1
Walthamstow Avenue vs Tooting & Mitcham United	1-1
Walton & Hersham vs Enfield	0-1
West Auckland Town vs Fareham Town	2-0
Wimbledon vs Windsor & Eton	2-1
Wycombe Wanderers vs Whitley Bay	4-2

Second Round Replays

Crook Town vs Hayes	3-1
Sutton United vs Bromley	3-0
Tooting & Mitcham United vs Walthamstow Avenue	2-2

Second Round Second Replay

Tooting & Mitcham United vs Walthamstow Avenue (at Tooting)	1-1

Second Round Third Replay

Walthamstow Avenue vs Tooting & Mitcham United (at Walthamstow)	3-1

Third Round

Barnet vs Sutton United	2-2
Carshalton Athletic vs Walthamstow Avenue	1-1
Eastwood Town vs Whitby Town	0-2
Enfield vs Wimbledon	2-0
Evenwood Town vs Ferryhill Athletic	0-3
Grays Athletic vs Kingstonian	1-2
West Auckland Town vs Crook Town	0-0
Wycombe Wanderers vs Spennymoor United	2-2

Third Round Replays

Crook Town vs West Auckland Town	1-0
Spennymoor United vs Wycombe Wanderers	2-1
Sutton United vs Barnet	1-2
Walthamstow Avenue vs Carshalton Athletic	2-1

Fourth Round

Enfield vs Whitby Town	3-0
Ferryhill Athletic vs Kingstonian	0-1
Spennymoor United vs Barnet	2-5
Walthamstow Avenue vs Crook Town	1-1

Fourth Round Replay

Crook Town vs Walthamstow Avenue	3-0

Semi-Finals

Crook Town vs Barnet (at Newcastle)	2-1
Kingstonian vs Enfield (at Chelsea)	0-0

Semi-Final Replay

Kingstonian vs Enfield (at Fulham)	2-3

Final

Enfield vs Crook Town	1-2

(at Wembley Stadium 18 April 1964)
Attendance: 37,000

Crook Town: Snowball, McCourt, Reid, Storey, Garbutt, Brown, Weir, Goodfellow, Lumsden, Roughley, McMillan
Scorers: Goodfellow, Brown
Enfield: Mitchell, Neale, Harris, D'Arcy, Kingsland, Cantwell, Thomas, Broomfield, Edwards, Day, Howard
Scorer: Day
Referee: D.W. Smith (Stonehouse)

1964-65 Amateur Cup

First Round

Alvechurch vs Norton Woodseats	2-0
Aveley vs Dulwich Hamlet	0-1
Bishop Auckland vs Loughborough Colleges	2-1
Callenders Athletic vs Kingstonian	0-10
Corinthian Casuals vs Harwich & Parkeston	0-1
Crook Town vs Willington	0-1
Croydon Amateurs vs Clapton	1-1
Eastbourne vs Leatherhead	2-1
Eastwood Town vs Evenwood Town	2-1
Enfield vs Dagenham	3-2
Fareham Town vs Carshalton Athletic	1-2
Ford United vs Maidenhead United	2-2
Hayes vs Harrow Town	4-4*, 3-1
* Harrow Town fielded a suspended player	
Hitchin Town vs Devizes Town	5-0
Hounslow vs Alton Town	10-0
Ilford vs Bishop's Stortford	0-2
Leytonstone vs Wycombe Wanderers	2-2
Maidstone United vs Barnet	1-4
Oxford City vs Southall	6-0
Spennymoor United vs Skelmersdale United	3-0
Stowmarket vs St. Albans City	0-1
Sutton United vs Hendon	1-2
Thackley vs Penrith	0-2
Tooting & Mitcham United vs Walthamstow Avenue	1-1
Tow Law Town vs Ferryhill Athletic	1-2
Walton & Hersham vs Torpoint Athletic	1-1
Wealdstone vs Grays Athletic	3-0
Whitby Town vs Moor Green	3-2
Whitley Bay vs West Auckland Town	4-3
Windsor & Eton vs Finchley	1-1
Woking vs Bromley	2-2
Yorkshire Amateurs vs Prestwich Heys	2-3

First Round Replays

Bromley vs Woking	2-1
Clapton vs Croydon Amateurs	0-1

Finchley vs Windsor & Eton	5-1
Maidenhead United vs Ford United	3-1
Torpoint Athletic vs Walton & Hersham	4-2
Walthamstow Avenue vs Tooting & Mitcham United	1-0
Wycombe Wanderers vs Leytonstone	0-2

Second Round

Alvechurch vs Walthamstow Avenue	2-1
Bishop Auckland vs Wealdstone	2-4
Bishop's Stortford vs Maidenhead United	4-1
Carshalton Athletic vs Hounslow	4-1
Croydon Amateurs vs St. Albans City	1-2
Dulwich Hamlet vs Whitley Bay	1-2
Eastbourne vs Whitby Town	0-2
Eastwood Town vs Prestwich Heys	5-3
Enfield vs Barnet	1-1
Finchley vs Hayes	4-0
Hendon vs Leytonstone	5-1
Hitchin Town vs Oxford City	2-2
Kingstonian vs Spennymoor United	11-2
Penrith vs Ferryhill Athletic	1-3
Torpoint Athletic vs Harwich & Parkeston	0-4
Willington vs Bromley	2-4

Second Round Replays

| Barnet vs Enfield | 2-3 |
| Oxford City vs Hitchin Town | 3-1 |

Third Round

Alvechurch vs Wealdstone	4-1
Bromley vs Kingstonian	0-0
Eastwood Town vs Enfield	2-3
Ferryhill Athletic vs Finchley	1-2
Harwich & Parkeston vs Bishop's Stortford	0-0
Hendon vs Carshalton Athletic	5-1
Oxford City vs Whitby Town	1-2
St. Albans City vs Whitley Bay	0-1

Third Round Replays

| Bishop's Stortford vs Harwich & Parkeston | 1-2 |
| Kingstonian vs Bromley | 4-2 |

Fourth Round

Alvechurch vs Enfield	1-3
Harwich & Parkeston vs Whitby Town	0-0
Kingstonian vs Finchley	0-2
Whitley Bay vs Hendon	1-3

Fourth Round Replay

| Whitby Town vs Harwich & Parkeston | 3-2 |

Semi-Finals

Hendon vs Finchley	4-1
(at Highbury)	
Whitby Town vs Enfield	2-1
(at Sunderland)	

Final

| Hendon vs Whitby Town | 3-1 |

(at Wembley Stadium 24 April 1965)

Attendance: 45,000

Hendon: Swannell, Hogwood, Sleap, Evans, Riddy, Cantwell, Drake, Slade, Hyde, Quail, Lakey
Scorers: Hyde 2, Quail
Whitby Town: Pybus, Durnall, Hobbs, Kennerley, Barker, Moody, Geldart, Edwards, Mulvaney, McHale, Crostwaite
Scorer: Mulvaney
Referee: G. McCabe (Sheffield)

1965-66 Amateur Cup

First Round

Bishop's Stortford vs Herne Bay	1-0
Bromley vs Walthamstow Avenue	2-1
Corinthian Casuals vs Torpoint Athletic	3-0
Dagenham vs Harlow Town	1-0
Enfield vs Walton & Hersham	5-1
Fareham Town vs St. Albans City	1-2
Ferndale Y.C. vs Carshalton Athletic	0-7
Ferryhill Athletic vs Evenwood Town	4-2
Finchley vs Dulwich Hamlet	2-0
Gosport Borough Athletic vs Eastbourne	1-2
Hayes vs Grays Athletic	3-3
Hendon vs Harwich & Parkeston	3-1
Lancing vs Kingstonian	0-3
Leyton vs Hemel Hempstead	2-2
Leytonstone vs Tooting & Mitcham United	4-2
Loughborough Colleges vs Norton Woodseats	3-0
Maidenhead United vs Windsor & Eton	3-0
Maidstone United vs Barking	1-2
Moor Green vs Crook Town	1-2
Oxford City vs Leatherhead	2-3
Skelmersdale United vs Alvechurch	0-2
Spennymoor United vs Eastwood Town	1-1
Stanley United vs Penrith	0-2
Stowmarket vs Woking	3-2
Sutton United vs Clapton	7-0
Wealdstone vs Hitchin Town	4-1
West Auckland Town vs Prestwich Heys	4-2
Whitby Town vs Bishop Auckland	1-3
Willington vs Tow Law Town	1-3
Witney Town vs Hounslow	2-1
Wycombe Wanderers vs Aveley	2-1

Yorkshire Amateurs vs Whitley Bay — 1-2

First Round Replays

Eastwood Town vs Spennymoor United	2-3
Grays Athletic vs Hayes	1-2
Hemel Hempstead vs Leyton	0-1

Second Round

Barking vs Ferryhill Athletic	3-0
Corinthian Casuals vs Hayes	1-2
Crook Town vs West Auckland Town	1-2
Eastbourne vs Enfield	2-3
Finchley vs Bishop Auckland	0-2
Hendon vs Carshalton Athletic	1-1
Leytonstone vs Bishop's Stortford	0-2
Loughborough Colleges vs Bromley	3-2
Maidenhead United vs Leatherhead	7-0
Spennymoor United vs Leyton	4-1
Stowmarket vs Alvechurch	4-2
Sutton United vs Dagenham	1-3
Wealdstone vs Tow Law Town	1-3
Whitley Bay vs Kingstonian	2-1
Witney Town vs St. Albans City	2-1
Wycombe Wanderers vs Penrith	1-2

Second Round Replays

Alvechurch vs Stowmarket	3-2
St. Albans City vs Witney Town	4-1

Third Round

Barking vs Wealdstone	1-3
Enfield vs Alvechurch	2-3
Hendon vs Leytonstone	2-1
Leatherhead vs Hayes	2-2
Leyton vs Whitley Bay	0-5
Loughborough Colleges vs Crook Town	1-2
Sutton United vs Bishop Auckland	2-1
Wycombe Wanderers vs St. Albans City	1-1

Third Round Replays

Hayes vs Leatherhead	0-1
St. Albans City vs Wycombe Wanderers	0-3

Fourth Round

Crook Town vs Alvechurch	0-2
Hendon vs Wycombe Wanderers	2-1
Wealdstone vs Leatherhead	2-1
Whitley Bay vs Sutton United	2-0

Semi-Finals

Wealdstone vs Alvechurch (at Chelsea)	1-0

Whitley Bay vs Hendon — 1-2
(at Sunderland)

Final

Hendon vs Wealdstone — 1-3
(at Wembley Stadium 16 April 1966)
Attendance: 45,000

Wealdstone: Goymer, Doyle, Sedgley, Townsend, Ashworth, Dillsworth, Allen, Childs, Cooley, Lindsay, Bremner
Scorers: Childs 2, Bremner
Hendon: Swannell, Hogwood, Cooper, Shacklock, Riddy, Cantwell, Churchill, Evans, Swain, Sleap, Hyde
Scorer: Riddy
Referee: N. Burtenshaw (Norfolk)

1966-67 Amateur Cup

First Round

Addlestone vs Windsor & Eton	2-2
Barking vs Woking	1-2
Bromley vs Corinthian Casuals	2-1
Brook Sports vs Whitby Town	1-0
Bristol St. George vs Dagenham	1-0
Cambridge University vs Wembley	1-1
Crook Town vs Loughborough Colleges	1-2
Eastbourne vs Oxford City	0-3
Enfield vs Sutton United	3-0
Evenwood Town vs Highgate United	0-2
Ferryhill Athletic vs Prestwich Heys	1-1
Grays Athletic vs Dulwich Hamlet	2-2
Hallam vs Whitley Bay	0-3
Hayes vs Gosport Borough Athletic	0-4
Hoddesdon vs Clapton	0-0
Hounslow vs Harwich & Parkeston	2-3
Ilford vs Hendon	0-3
Kingstonian vs Carshalton Athletic	2-0
Leatherhead vs Bishop's Stortford	1-1
Leyton vs Torpoint Athletic	1-1
Leytonstone vs Wycombe Wanderers	4-2
North Shields vs Alvechurch	3-0
Penrith vs Eastwood Town	1-3
Skelmersdale United vs Bishop Auckland	3-0
Slough Town vs Hitchin Town	1-1
Southall vs Maidenhead United	6-1
Spennymoor United vs Consett	1-1
Tow Law Town vs West Auckland Town	1-0
Vauxhall Motors vs Finchley	1-3
Walthamstow Avenue vs St. Albans City	2-0
Wealdstone vs Stowmarket	1-1
West Thurrock vs Fareham Town	1-4

First Round Replays

Bishop's Stortford vs Leatherhead	1-2
Clapton vs Hoddesdon	3-1
Consett vs Spennymoor United	2-0
Dulwich Hamlet vs Grays Athletic	0-2
Hitchin Town vs Slough Town	1-3
Prestwich Heys vs Ferryhill Athletic	4-0
Stowmarket vs Wealdstone	1-1
Torpoint Athletic vs Leyton	2-4
Wembley vs Cambridge University	5-2
Windsor & Eton vs Addlestone	3-2

First Round Second Replay

Wealdstone vs Stowmarket	5-2
(at Colchester)	

Second Round

Bristol St. George vs Hendon	0-0
Bromley vs Kingstonian	1-4
Brook Sports vs Wealdstone	0-3
Clapton vs Fareham Town	2-0
Consett vs Gosport Borough Athletic	1-5
Harwich & Parkeston vs Slough Town	0-2
Highgate United vs Eastwood Town	2-1
Leytonstone vs Grays Athletic	5-1
Oxford City vs North Shields	0-0
Prestwich Heys vs Finchley	3-1
Skelmersdale United vs Leyton	3-0
Southall vs Woking	2-1
Tow Law Town vs Leatherhead	0-1
Wembley vs Enfield	1-2
Whitley Bay vs Loughborough Colleges	4-1
Windsor & Eton vs Walthamstow Avenue	3-3

Second Round Replays

Hendon vs Bristol St. George	5-0
North Shields vs Oxford City	1-1
Walthamstow Avenue vs Windsor & Eton	5-0

Second Round Second Replay

Oxford City vs North Shields	4-3
(at Doncaster)	

Third Round

Clapton vs Leatherhead	2-3
Hendon vs Oxford City	4-3
Kingstonian vs Gosport Borough Athletic	4-0
Leytonstone vs Enfield	1-1
Prestwich Heys vs Highgate United	1-2
Southall vs Slough Town	0-1
Skelmersdale United vs Wealdstone	1-0
Whitley Bay vs Walthamstow Avenue	0-2

Third Round Replay

Enfield vs Leytonstone	1-0

Fourth Round

Highgate United vs Enfield	0-1*, 0-6
* match abandoned	
Leatherhead vs Hendon	0-3
Slough Town vs Skelmersdale United	2-2
Walthamstow Avenue vs Kingstonian	5-0

Fourth Round Replay

Skelmersdale United vs Slough Town	1-0

Semi-Finals

Enfield vs Walthamstow Avenue	1-0
(at Crystal Palace)	
Skelmersdale United vs Hendon	0-0
(at Derby)	

Semi-Final Replay

Skelmersdale United vs Hendon	2-2
(at St. Andrew's, Birmingham)	

Semi-Final Second Replay

Skelmersdale United vs Hendon	3-1
(at West Bromwich)	

Final

Enfield vs Skelmersdale United	0-0
(at Wembley Stadium 22 April 1967)	

Attendance: 75,000

Enfield: Wolstenholme, Sedgley, Reid, Payne, D'Arcy, Moxon, Churchill, Connell, Hill, Day, Howard. **Sub**: Adams
Skelmersdale United: Crosbie, Bermingham, Bridge, Unsworth, Wade, Moorcroft, Whitehead, Worswick, Bennett, Burns, Mansley. **Sub**: McDermott
Referee: E.T. Jennings (Stourbridge)

Final Replay

Skelmersdale United vs Enfield	0-3
(at Maine Road, Manchester 29 April 1967)	

Attendance: 55,388

Enfield: Wolstenholme, Sedgley, Reid, Payne, D'Arcy, Moxon, Churchill, Connell, Hill, Day, Adams. **Sub**: Howard
Scorers: Connell, Hill 2
Skelmersdale United: Crosbie, Bermingham, McDermott, Unsworth, Wade, Moorcroft, Whitehead, Worswick, Bennett, Burns, Mansley. **Sub**: Felmingham
Referee: E.T. Jennings (Stourbridge)

1967-68 Amateur Cup

First Round

Alvechurch vs Tow Law Town	1-2
Barking vs Hendon	1-0
Bishop's Stortford vs Walthamstow Avenue	5-3
Bristol St. George vs Leyton	3-1
Bromley vs Walton & Hersham	0-0
Carshalton Athletic vs Kingstonian	2-2
Chesham United vs Maidenhead United	2-2
City of Norwich Old Boys Union versus	
Wycombe Wanderers	1-0
Clapton vs Leytonstone	0-2
Corinthian Casuals vs Hounslow	4-1
Coventry Amateurs vs Hallam	2-1
Cray Wanderers vs Eastbourne	4-1
Crook Town vs Evenwood Town	1-2
Eastwood Town vs Bishop Auckland	1-0
Harwich & Parkeston vs Fareham Town	1-0
Hayes vs Grays Athletic	3-0
Hitchin Town vs Sutton United	1-2
Ilford vs Lewes	1-2
Leatherhead vs Dagenham	1-2
Marine vs Ferryhill Athletic	3-1
North Shields vs Ossett Albion	3-0
Norton Woodseats vs Whitley Bay	0-2
Penrith vs Prestwich Heys	1-2
St. Albans City vs Oxford City	1-2
Sharpness vs Dulwich Hamlet	1-2
Skelmersdale United vs Spennymoor United	0-1
Slough Town vs Finchley	3-2
Southall vs Woking	2-0
Tilbury vs Gosport Borough Athletic	2-0
Torpoint Athletic vs Wealdstone	2-4
West Auckland Town vs Loughborough Colleges	2-2
Windsor & Eton vs Enfield	1-3

First Round Replays

Kingstonian vs Carshalton Athletic	4-3
Loughborough Colleges vs West Auckland Town	0-1
Maidenhead United vs Chesham United	2-2
Walton & Hersham vs Bromley	3-1

First Round Second Replay

Chesham United vs Maidenhead United	2-1
(at Wycombe Wanderers)	

Second Round

Barking vs Coventry Amateurs	3-0
Bishop's Stortford vs Bristol St. George	3-1
Dulwich Hamlet vs Chesham United	1-1
Eastwood Town vs Whitley Bay	1-0
Evenwood Town vs Sutton United	0-0

Harwich & Parkeston vs Corinthian Casuals	0-1
Hayes vs Cray Wanderers	0-0
Lewes vs Tilbury	3-4
Leytonstone vs Southall	1-0
Marine vs City of Norwich Old Boys Union	2-1
North Shields vs Enfield	2-3
Oxford City vs Tow Law Town	2-1
Spennymoor United vs Prestwich Heys	1-1
Walton & Hersham vs Dagenham	1-2
Wealdstone vs Kingstonian	2-0
West Auckland Town vs Slough Town	1-3

Second Round Replays

Chesham United vs Dulwich Hamlet	4-2
Crays Wanderers vs Hayes	1-0
Prestwich Heys vs Spennymoor United	2-1
Sutton United vs Evenwood Town	3-0

Third Round

Corinthian Casuals vs Chesham United	0-0
Cray Wanderers vs Barking	0-0
Dagenham vs Marine	0-0
Eastwood Town vs Wealdstone	1-1
Leytonstone vs Bishop's Stortford	7-2
Oxford City vs Prestwich Heys	4-2
Slough Town vs Sutton United	1-1
Tilbury vs Enfield	0-2

Third Round Replays

Barking vs Cray Wanderers	2-0
Chesham United vs Corinthian Casuals	1-0
Marine vs Dagenham	3-4
Sutton United vs Slough Town	1-0
Wealdstone vs Eastwood Town	4-1

Fourth Round

Enfield vs Leytonstone	0-0
Oxford City vs Chesham United	0-0
Sutton United vs Dagenham	2-1
Wealdstone vs Barking	3-1

Fourth Round Replays

Chesham United vs Oxford City	2-0
Leytonstone vs Enfield	0-0

Fourth Round Second Replay

Enfield vs Leytonstone	0-1
(at Brisbane Road)	

Semi-Finals

Sutton United vs Leytonstone	0-0
(at Crystal Palace)	

Wealdstone vs Chesham United 0-2
(at Fulham)

Semi-Final Replay

Sutton United vs Leytonstone 1-3
(at Brentford)

Final

Leytonstone vs Chesham United 1-0
(at Wembley Stadium 20 April 1968)

Attendance: 52,000

Leytonstone: Hadlow, Tilley, Hames, Andrews, Thomson, Walker, Charles, Gray, Diwell, Minall, Harvey. **Sub**: Albon
Scorer: Gray
Chesham United: Wells, Thackray, Smith, Caterer, Burgess, McCaffrey, Ellis, Black, Fruen, Harper, Kent
Sub: Frost
Referee: F. Cowen (Lancashire)

1968-69 Amateur Cup

First Round

Alton Town vs Croydon Amateurs	3-0
Carshalton Athletic vs Finchley	2-1
Chesham United vs Walthamstow Avenue	0-2
Coventry Amateurs vs Eastwood Town	1-1
Dagenham vs Windsor & Eton	4-0
Dulwich Hamlet vs Corinthian Casuals	1-1
Emley vs Evenwood Town	2-1
Enfield vs Leatherhead	0-0
Fareham Town vs Cirencester Town	1-1
Grays Athletic vs Barking	1-1
Hayes vs Bristol St. George	2-1
Hendon vs Hornchurch	2-0
Hertford Town vs Wealdstone	0-0
Hitchin Town vs Stowmarket	2-0
Ilford vs Cheshunt	0-1
Kingstonian vs Southall	1-1
Leeds & Carnegie College vs Billingham Synthonia	2-1
Lincoln United vs Crook Town	2-1
Marine vs West Auckland Town	2-2
Melksham Town vs Harwich & Parkeston	2-3
North Shields vs Spennymoor United	4-1
Oxford City vs Wycombe Wanderers	3-2
St. Albans City vs Bishop's Stortford	3-0
Skelmersdale United vs Hallam	3-0
Sutton United vs Bromley	9-0
Torpoint Athletic vs Cray Wanderers	1-3
Tow Law Town vs Alvechurch	3-1
Walton & Hersham vs Slough Town	2-2
Wembley vs Leyton	1-0

Whitby Town vs Guinness Exports	1-0
Whitley Bay vs Prestwich Heys	1-0
Woking vs Leytonstone	0-1

First Round Replays

Barking vs Grays Athletic	5-0
Cirencester Town vs Fareham Town	3-1
Corinthian Casuals vs Dulwich Hamlet	1-2
Eastwood Town vs Coventry Amateurs	1-3
Leatherhead vs Enfield	1-1
Slough Town vs Walton & Hersham	2-1
Southall vs Kingstonian	0-4
Wealdstone vs Hertford Town	3-3
West Auckland Town vs Marine	0-2

First Round Second Replays

Enfield vs Leatherhead	1-0
(at Dulwich Hamlet)	
Wealdstone vs Hertford Town	1-1
(at Wealdstone)	

First Round Third Replay

Wealdstone vs Hertford Town	1-1
(at Wembley F.C.)	

First Round Fourth Replay

Hertford Town vs Wealdstone	0-1
(at Hertford)	

Second Round

Alton Town vs Whitley Bay	0-2
Barking vs Wembley	4-1
Carshalton Athletic vs Whitby Town	2-2
Cheshunt vs Enfield	0-0
Cray Wanderers vs Leytonstone	2-2
Dagenham vs Harwich & Parkeston	0-1
Emley vs Dulwich Hamlet	1-0
Hayes vs Tow Law Town	2-0
Kingstonian vs Lincoln United	2-0
Leeds & Carnegie College vs Sutton United	2-5
Marine vs Walthamstow Avenue	2-0
North Shields vs Coventry Amateurs	3-0
St. Albans City vs Hendon	0-2
Skelmersdale United vs Oxford City	1-1
Slough Town vs Hitchin Town	4-0
Wealdstone vs Cirencester Town	3-1

Second Round Replays

Enfield vs Cheshunt	2-1
Leytonstone vs Cray Wanderers	2-0
Oxford City vs Skelmersdale United	1-3
Whitby Town vs Carshalton Athletic	1-0

Third Round

Emley vs Barking	0-2*, 0-1
* match abandoned	
Harwich & Parkeston vs Enfield	1-1
Leytonstone vs Kingstonian	1-0
North Shields vs Hendon	1-1
Skelmersdale United vs Whitby Town	3-1
Sutton United vs Marine	2-0
Wealdstone vs Hayes	1-0
Whitley Bay vs Slough Town	3-2

Third Round Replays

Enfield vs Harwich & Parkeston	4-0
Hendon vs North Shields	0-2

Fourth Round

Enfield vs Skelmersdale United	1-2
North Shields vs Wealdstone	1-0
Sutton United vs Leytonstone	3-1
Whitley Bay vs Barking	5-1

Semi-Finals

North Shields vs Skelmersdale United	1-1
(at Middlesbrough)	
Sutton United vs Whitley Bay	4-2
(at St. Andrew's Birmingham)	

Semi-Final Replay

Skelmersdale United vs North Shields	1-2
(at Southport)	

Final

Sutton United vs North Shields	1-2
(at Wembley Stadium 12 April 1969)	

Attendance: 47,500

North Shields: Morgan, Driver, Twaddle, Hall, Tatum, Thompson, Wrightson, Lister, Joicey, Cassidy, Rutherford
Sub: Orrick
Scorers: Hall, Joicey
Sutton United: Roffey, Garfield, Grose, Brookes, Clarke, Gradi, Bladon, Mellows, Drabwell, Pritchard, Howard
Sub: Gane
Scorer: Mellows
Referee: P.R. Walters (Somerset)

1969-70 Amateur Cup

First Round

Alton Town vs Walthamstow Avenue	5-0
Aveley vs Kingstonian	1-0
Bishop's Stortford vs Dulwich Hamlet	5-2
Bristol St. George vs Fareham Town	4-2
Bromley vs Oxford City	3-2
Carshalton Athletic vs Hitchin Town	0-0
Chesham United vs Slough Town	2-3
Cheshunt vs Windsor & Eton	3-1
Coventry Amateurs vs West Auckland Town	1-2
Croydon Amateurs vs Wycombe Wanderers	0-1
Durham City vs Skelmersdale United	1-1
Eastwood Town vs Leeds & Carnegie College	0-2
Enfield vs Redhill	3-2
Gorleston vs Southall	1-4
Evesham United vs Cray Wanderers	1-0
Guinness Exports vs Emley	0-3
Harwich & Parkeston vs Leyton	9-0
Hayes vs Barking	0-2
Hendon vs St. Austell	5-0
Hoddesdon Town vs Dagenham	1-2
Ilford vs Witney Town	1-0
North Shields vs Evenwood Town	0-0
Paget Rangers vs Alvechurch	1-1
Prestwich Heys vs Marine	1-0
St. Albans City vs Wembley	0-0
St. John's College, York vs Whitley Bay	0-1
(at Whitley Bay)	
Sutton United vs Leatherhead	2-0
Tooting & Mitcham United vs Leytonstone	0-0
Tow Law Town vs Spennymoor United	1-0
Wealdstone vs Vauxhall Motors	3-2
Whitby Town vs Loughborough Colleges	1-1
Woking vs Walton & Hersham	0-0

First Round Replays

Alvechurch vs Paget Rangers	2-2
Evenwood Town vs North Shields	0-0
Hitchin Town vs Carshalton Athletic	3-0
Leytonstone vs Tooting & Mitcham United	0-1
Loughborough Colleges vs Whitby Town	0-2
Skelmersdale United vs Durham City	3-2
Walton & Hersham vs Woking	2-1
Wembley vs St. Albans City	1-1

First Round Second Replays

Alvechurch vs Paget Rangers	3-1
(at St. Andrew's)	
Evenwood Town vs North Shields	3-1
(at Hartlepool)	
St. Albans City vs Wembley	2-1
(at St. Albans)	

Second Round

Alton Town vs Hitchin Town	2-1
Alvechurch vs Whitby Town	3-0
Bishop's Stortford vs Skelmersdale United	0-4

Cheshunt vs Ilford	3-2
Dagenham vs Barking	1-1
Evenwood Town vs Hendon	1-2*, 1-1
* match abandoned	
Harwich & Parkeston vs St. Albans City	1-3
Leeds & Carnegie College vs Walton & Hersham	0-4
Prestwich Heys vs Sutton United	3-1
Slough Town vs Aveley	2-0
Southall vs Bristol St. George	2-2
Tow Law Town vs Evesham United	1-0
Wealdstone vs Bromley	3-2
West Auckland Town vs Emley	0-1
Whitley Bay vs Enfield	0-0
Wycombe Wanderers vs Tooting & Mitcham United	0-0

Second Round Replays

Barking vs Dagenham	1-3
Bristol St. George vs Southall	2-5
Enfield vs Whitley Bay	4-1
Hendon vs Evenwood Town	4-2
Tooting & Mitcham United vs Wycombe Wanderers	1-2

Third Round

Alton Town vs Enfield	2-5
Alvechurch vs Slough Town	2-2
Emley vs Dagenham	0-0
Hendon vs Walton & Hersham	1-1
Prestwich Heys vs Southall	1-0
St. Albans City vs Tow Law Town	4-0
Skelmersdale United vs Cheshunt	1-0
Wealdstone vs Wycombe Wanderers	0-1

Third Round Replays

Dagenham vs Emley	5-0
Slough Town vs Alvechurch	2-0
Walton & Hersham vs Hendon	1-0

Fourth Round

Enfield vs Prestwich Heys	2-0
Slough Town vs Skelmersdale United	0-0
Walton & Hersham vs Dagenham	0-1
Wycombe Wanderers vs St. Albans City	0-2

Semi-Finals

Enfield vs Skelmersdale United	1-0
(at Derby)	
Dagenham vs St. Albans City	1-1
(at Millwall)	

Semi-Final Replay

| Dagenham vs St. Albans City | 1-0 |
| (at Luton) | |

Final

| Enfield vs Dagenham | 5-1 |

(at Wembley Stadium 4 April 1970)

Attendance: 33,000

Enfield: Wolstenholme, Clayton, Payne, Betson, Day, Adams, Connell, Feely, Gray, Hill. **Sub**: D'Arcy
Scorers: Connell 2, Feely, Adams, Daniels (own goal)
Dagenham: Huttley, Robertson, Dudley, Daniels, Still, Moore, Leakey, Drake, M. Smith, B. Smith, Brookes
Sub: Scarfe
Scorer: Brookes
Referee: D. J. Lydon (Birmingham)

1970-71 Amateur Cup

First Round

Alton Town vs Hendon	1-1
Alvechurch vs Ormskirk	0-1
Barking vs Paulton Rovers	4-1
Bracknell Town vs Newquay	0-2
Bristol St. George vs Boreham Wood	0-3
Bromley vs St. Albans City	3-3
Carshalton Athletic vs Cheshunt	2-1
Cray Wanderers vs Kingstonian	1-2
Croydon Amateurs vs Harwich & Parkeston	1-4
Dagenham vs Leyton	5-0
Durham City vs Whitley Bay	2-3
Fareham Town vs Tooting & Mitcham United	1-3
Finchley vs Woking	2-1
Irlam Town vs Oldbury United	1-2
Leeds & Carnegie College vs Loughborough Colleges	0-2
Marine vs Prestwich Heys	2-1
Oxford City vs Bishop's Stortford	1-3
Slough Town vs Redhill	1-1
Southall vs Dulwich Hamlet	2-3
South Bank vs North Shields	1-3
Spennymoor United vs Skelmersdale United	1-1
Stowmarket vs Leatherhead	2-2
Sutton Coldfield Town vs Emley	4-0
Sutton United vs Leytonstone	0-0
Tilbury vs Aveley	0-1
Tow Law Town vs West Auckland Town	2-1
Vauxhall Motors vs Hayes	0-3
Walthamstow Avenue vs Ilford	2-0
Walton & Hersham vs Enfield	0-2
Whitby Town vs Evenwood Town	2-3
Witney Town vs Hitchin Town	2-1
Wycombe Wanderers vs Wealdstone	1-0

First Round Replays

| Hendon vs Alton Town | 6-0 |
| Leatherhead vs Stowmarket | 2-2 |

Leytonstone vs Sutton United	4-0
Redhill vs Slough Town	1-3
St. Albans City vs Bromley	4-0
Skelmersdale United vs Spennymoor United	5-1

First Round Second Replay

Leatherhead vs Stowmarket	3-2
(at Enfield)	

Second Round

Bishop's Stortford vs Dagenham	0-1
Boreham Wood vs St. Albans City	2-1
Carshalton Athletic vs Aveley	2-3
Harwich & Parkeston vs Slough Town	0-3
Hayes vs Witney Town	2-1
Hendon vs Barking	4-1
Leatherhead vs Dulwich Hamlet	0-0
Leytonstone vs Kingstonian	4-1
Loughborough Colleges vs Evenwood Town	1-0
Marine vs Ormskirk	3-1
Newquay vs Oldbury United	1-7
North Shields vs Tow Law Town	0-0
Skelmersdale United vs Sutton Coldfield Town	3-0
Tooting & Mitcham United vs Walthamstow Avenue	3-1
Whitley Bay vs Finchley	2-0
Wycombe Wanderers vs Enfield	2-1

Second Round Replays

Dulwich Hamlet vs Leatherhead	0-1
Tow Law Town vs North Shields	6-0

Third Round

Boreham Wood vs Leatherhead	1-1
Hendon vs Slough Town	1-1
Leytonstone vs Dagenham	0-1
Loughborough Colleges vs Hayes	0-3
Marine vs Aveley	0-1
Tooting & Mitcham United vs Whitley Bay	2-3
Tow Law Town vs Skelmersdale United	1-1
Wycombe Wanderers vs Oldbury United	4-0

Third Round Replays

Leatherhead vs Boreham Wood	2-1
Skelmersdale United vs Tow Law Town	1-0
Slough Town vs Hendon	3-1

Fourth Round

Aveley vs Slough Town	0-2
Dagenham vs Whitley Bay	1-0
Hayes vs Leatherhead	1-1
Wycombe Wanderers vs Skelmersdale United	0-3

Fourth Round Replay

Leatherhead vs Hayes	1-0

Semi-Finals

Dagenham vs Slough Town	3-3
(at Charlton)	
Skelmersdale United vs Leatherhead	2-0
(at Bolton)	

Semi-Final Replay

Slough Town vs Dagenham	1-2
(at Fulham)	

Final

Dagenham vs Skelmersdale United	1-4
(at Wembley Stadium 24 April 1971)	

Attendance: 45,000

Skelmersdale United: Frankish, Allan, Poole, Turner, Bennett, McDermott, Swift, Wolfe, Dickin, Hardcastle, Clements. **Sub:** Windsor
Scorers: Dickin 3, Windsor
Dagenham: Huttley, Ford, Dudley, Davidson, Still, Moore, Leakey, Fry, Bass, Baker, Dear. **Sub:** M. Smith
Scorer: Bass
Referee: R. Tinkler (Boston)

1971-72 Amateur Cup

First Round

Alvechurch vs Blyth Spartans	0-1
Aveley vs Wycombe Wanderers	2-2
Bristol St. George vs Finchley	1-2
Bromley vs Oxford City	1-2
Cheshunt vs Tilbury	1-1
Corinthian Casuals vs Maidenhead United	0-1
(at Sutton)	
Croydon Amateurs vs Wantage Town	4-0
Evenwood Town vs Oldbury United	3-3
Evesham United vs Prestwich Heys	2-1
Hallam vs North Shields	0-1
Harwich & Parkeston vs St. Albans City	1-1
Hayes vs City of Norwich Old Boys Union	5-1
Hendon vs Horsham	1-0
Hitchin Town vs Erith & Belvedere	0-0
Ilford vs Bognor Regis Town	4-0
Leatherhead vs Dagenham	2-1
Letchworth Town vs Cadbury Heath	1-1
Leytonstone vs Carshalton Avenue	1-0
Loughborough Colleges vs Whitby Town	4-0
Marine vs Whitley Bay	4-1

Ruislip Manor vs Bishop's Stortford	2-2
Shildon vs Ormskirk	1-1
Slough Town vs Kingstonian	2-0
Spennymoor United vs Emley	5-0
Tooting & Mitcham United vs Barking	1-2
Tow Law Town vs Leeds & Carnegie College	1-1
Walthamstow Avenue vs Enfield	1-3
Walton & Hersham vs Southall	1-1
West Auckland Town vs Highgate United	1-4
Witney Town vs Dulwich Hamlet	2-1

First Round Replays

Bishop's Stortford vs Ruislip Manor	1-0
Cadbury Heath vs Letchworth Town	2-1
Erith & Belvedere vs Hitchin Town	1-3
Leeds & Carnegie College vs Tow Law Town	0-3
Oldbury United vs Evenwood Town	1-1
Ormskirk vs Shildon	1-3
St. Albans City vs Harwich & Parkeston	4-0
Southall vs Walton & Hersham	0-1
Tilbury vs Cheshunt	3-2
Wycombe Wanderers vs Aveley	5-1

First Round Second Replay

Evenwood Town vs Oldbury United	1-2
(at Bradford)	

Second Round

Barking vs Hayes	1-2
Cadbury Heath vs Walton & Hersham	0-1
Enfield vs Evesham United	3-1
Finchley v Bishop's Stortford	0-0
Highgate United vs Hendon	1-1
Hitchin Town vs Shildon	1-0
Ilford vs Maidenhead United	1-2
Leytonstone vs Loughborough Colleges	1-1
Oxford City vs Leatherhead	0-3
Slough Town vs St. Albans City	3-2
Sutton United vs Oldbury United	3-1
Tilbury vs Croydon Amateurs	1-1
Tow Law Town vs Blyth Spartans	0-4
Witney Town vs Marine	2-2
Woking vs North Shields	1-0
Wycombe Wanderers vs Spennymoor United	2-1

Second Round Replays

Bishop's Stortford vs Finchley	2-0
Croydon Amateurs vs Tilbury	3-2
Hendon vs Highgate United	2-1
Loughborough Colleges vs Leytonstone	1-4
Marine vs Witney Town	2-0

Third Round

Bishop's Stortford vs Hitchin Town	1-1
Hayes vs Croydon Amateurs	3-1
Hendon vs Maidenhead United	0-0
Leytonstone vs Leatherhead	2-2
Marine vs Enfield	0-3
Slough Town vs Sutton United	1-0
Walton & Hersham vs Wycombe Wanderers	1-2
Woking vs Blyth Spartans	0-3

Third Round Replays

Hitchin Town vs Bishop's Stortford	2-2
Leatherhead vs Leytonstone	3-0
Maidenhead United vs Hendon	0-1

Third Round Second Replay

Bishop's Stortford vs Hitchin Town	2-2
(at Hertford)	

Third Round Third Replay

Hitchin Town vs Bishop's Stortford	1-0
(at St. Albans)	

Fourth Round

Blyth Spartans vs Leatherhead	1-1
Enfield vs Slough Town	5-1
Hendon vs Hitchin Town	2-0
Wycombe Wanderers vs Hayes	1-0

Fourth Round Replay

Leatherhead vs Blyth Spartans	0-1

Semi-Finals

Blyth Spartans vs Enfield	0-2
(at Newcastle)	
Wycombe Wanderers vs Hendon	1-2
(at Brentford)	

Final

Enfield vs Hendon	0-2
(at Wembley Stadium 22 April 1972)	

Attendance: 38,000

Hendon: Swannell, Jennings, Hand, Deadman, Phillips, Haider, Childs, Connell, Bass, Baker, Jameson.
Sub: Moore
Scorers: Smith (own goal), Bass
Enfield: Williams, Gibson, Hill, Payne, Betson, Smith, Albom, Adams, Butterfield, Gray, Turley. **Sub**: Brooks
Referee: E.D. Wallace (Swindon)

1972-73 Amateur Cup

First Round

Ashington vs Alvechurch	0-1
Aveley vs Wembley	3-1
Barking vs Shillington	3-0
Bishop Auckland vs Sutton Coldfield Town	0-0
Bishop's Stortford vs Boreham Wood	1-0
Carshalton Athletic vs Harlow Town	0-2
Dagenham vs Walthamstow Avenue	2-1
Devizes Town vs Hitchin Town	1-4
Dulwich Hamlet vs Tooting & Mitcham United	1-4
Enfield vs Leytonstone	1-1
Evenwood Town vs Tow Law Town	3-0
Harwich & Parkeston vs Leatherhead	3-1
Hayes vs Tilbury	2-0
Hendon vs Chichester City	7-0
Highgate United vs Prescot Town	1-0
Hounslow vs Eastbourne Town	2-2
Ilford vs Fareham Town	2-0
Maidenhead Town vs Leyton	1-1
Marine vs Blyth Spartans	0-1
Ormskirk vs Loughborough Colleges	2-2
Ossett Albion vs Olbury United	1-1
Oxford City vs Woking	2-1
Paulton Rovers vs Croydon Amateurs	0-1
Prestwich Heys vs Leeds & Carnegie College	1-1
St. Albans City vs Finchley	0-0
Shildon vs Spennymoor United	0-1
Slough Town vs Cadbury Heath	2-1
Stowmarket vs Kingstonian	0-2
Sutton United vs Walton & Hersham	0-3
Whitley Bay vs North Shields	1-2
Witney Town vs Witham Town	5-0
Wycombe Wanderers vs Cheshunt	0-1

First Round Replays

Eastbourne United vs Hounslow	4-2*
* match abandoned during extra time	
Finchley vs St. Albans City	1-2
Leeds & Carnegie College vs Prestwich Heys	3-0
Leyton vs Maidenhead United	2-1
Leytonstone vs Enfield	3-2
Loughborough Colleges vs Ormskirk	1-2
Oldbury United vs Ossett Albion	1-0
Sutton Coldfield Town vs Bishop Auckland	0-2

First Round Second Replay

Eastbourne United vs Hounslow	1-0†, 4-0
† first match abandoned after 25 minutes	
(both matches played at Horsham)	

Second Round

Aveley vs Witney Town	0-0
Barking vs Evenwood Town	0-1
Bishop's Stortford vs Bishop Auckland	3-0
Blyth Spartans vs Hendon	1-1
Cheshunt vs Ormskirk	0-1
Croydon Amateurs vs Alvechurch	1-4
Dagenham vs Harwich & Parkeston	5-0
Eastbourne United vs Slough Town	0-2
Highgate United vs Tooting & Mitcham United	3-0
Hitchin Town vs Hayes	3-4
Ilford vs Kingstonian	2-1
Leeds & Carnegie College vs Walton & Hersham	0-3
Leyton vs Spennymoor United	0-3
Leytonstone vs Oldbury United	1-1
North Shields vs Oxford City	1-0
St. Albans City vs Harlow Town	2-0

Second Round Replays

Hendon vs Blyth Spartans	0-1
Oldbury United vs Leytonstone	0-0
Witney Town vs Aveley	1-3

Second Round Second Replay

Leytonstone vs Oldbury United	1-0
(at Oxford City)	

Third Round

Bishop's Stortford vs Aveley	1-0
Evenwood Town vs Alvechurch	3-1
Highgate United vs Ilford	3-0
North Shields vs Blyth Spartans	0-1
Ormskirk vs Dagenham	1-4
Slough Town vs Leytonstone	2-1
Spennymoor United vs Hayes	2-1
Walton & Hersham vs St. Albans City	5-0

Fourth Round

Dagenham vs Bishop's Stortford	1-1
Evenwood Town vs Highgate United	1-1
Slough Town vs Blyth Spartans	2-1
Walton & Hersham vs Spennymoor United	0-0

Fourth Round Replays

Bishop's Stortford vs Dagenham	2-1
Highgate United vs Evenwood Town	2-0
Spennymoor United vs Walton & Hersham	0-1

Semi-Finals

Bishop's Stortford vs Slough Town	0-1
(at Watford)	
Walton & Hersham vs Highgate United	0-0
(at Coventry)	

Semi-Final Replay

Walton & Hersham vs Highgate United	4-0
(at Crystal Palace)	

Final

Slough Town vs Walton & Hersham	0-1
(at Wembley Stadium 14 April 1973)	

Attendance: 41,000

Walton & Hersham: Teale, Thomas, Edwards, Bassett, Donaldson, Lambert, Woffinden, Connell, Smith, Morris, Somers. **Sub**: Foskett
Scorer: Connell
Slough Town: Wolstenholme, Reid, Eaton, Mead, D'Arcy, Reardon, Chatterton, Day, O'Sullivan, Gaine, Anthony
Sub: Jamieson
Referee: H.G. New (Gloucestershire)

1973-74 Amateur Cup

First Round

Aveley vs Alton Town	5-0
Bishop Auckland vs Shildon	0-3
Bishop's Stortford vs Hayes	2-0
Blyth Spartans vs Sutton Coldfield Town	3-0
Boreham Wood vs Hitchin Town	1-1
Cadbury Heath vs Tilbury	1-3
Chesham United vs Maidenhead United	3-2
Croydon vs Leyton	0-1
Dagenham vs Walton & Hersham	1-3
Dulwich Hamlet vs Newquay	3-0
Fareham Town vs Cheshunt	1-1
Faversham Town vs Barking	1-6
Hampton vs Leytonstone	2-4
Hendon vs Harwich & Parkeston	0-0
Hertford Town vs Finchley	2-0
Horsham vs Clacton Town	2-1
Kingstonian vs Ilford	0-0
Leatherhead vs Enfield	4-0
Leeds & Carnegie College vs Prestwich Heys	4-0
Loughborough Colleges vs Friar Lane Old Boys	2-2
Marine vs Ashington	1-2
Middlewich Athletic vs Oldbury United	4-0
North Shields vs Alvechurch	2-0
Ormskirk vs Evenwood Town	1-2
Oxford City vs Slough Town	1-1
St. Albans City vs Brockenhurst	1-1
Southall vs Carshalton Athletic	2-2
Spennymoor United vs Emley	4-0
Sutton United vs Tooting & Mitcham United	3-1
Tow Law Town vs Highgate United	1-2
Walthamstow Avenue vs Woking	1-2
Wycombe Wanderers vs Hornchurch	5-0

First Round Replays

Brockenhurst vs St. Albans City	2-0
Carshalton Athletic vs Southall	1-2
Cheshunt vs Fareham Town	1-1
Friar Lane Old Boys vs Loughborough Colleges	1-0
Harwich & Parkeston vs Hendon	1-1
Hitchin Town vs Boreham Wood	4-2
Ilford vs Kingstonian	2-1
Slough Town vs Oxford City	1-0

First Round Second Replays

Fareham Town vs Cheshunt	2-0
(at Maidenhead)	
Harwich & Parkeston vs Hendon	2-2
(at Colchester)	

First Round Third Replay

Hendon vs Harwich & Parkeston	2-0
(at Hendon)	

Second Round

Aveley vs Leyton	0-0
Barking vs Sutton United	1-3
Bishop's Stortford vs Hitchin Town	2-1
Blyth Spartans vs Fareham Town	2-0
Evenwood Town vs Wycombe Wanderers	0-3
Friar Lane Old Boys vs Chesham United	4-1
Highgate United vs Hertford Town	1-0
Horsham vs Woking	2-2
Ilford vs Brockenhurst	3-0
Leeds & Carnegie College vs Dulwich Hamlet	0-2
Leytonstone vs Walton & Hersham	0-1
Middlewich Athletic vs Leatherhead	0-9
North Shields vs Shildon	2-0
Slough Town vs Ashington	1-1
Southall vs Spennymoor United	1-1
Tilbury vs Hendon	0-0

Second Round Replays

Ashington vs Slough Town	1-0
Hendon vs Tilbury	2-0
Leyton vs Aveley	0-1
Spennymoor United vs Southall	4-1
Woking vs Horsham	3-2

Third Round

Ashington vs North Shields	1-1
Aveley vs Woking	1-1
Blyth Spartans vs Wycombe Wanderers	2-1
Dulwich Hamlet vs Friar Lane Old Boys	4-1
Hendon vs Leatherhead	1-1
Ilford vs Highgate United	2-1

Spennymoor United vs Sutton United	0-2
Walton & Hersham vs Bishop's Stortford	0-0

Third Round Replays

Bishop's Stortford vs Walton & Hersham	1-0
Leatherhead vs Hendon	1-1
North Shields vs Ashington	0-2
Woking vs Aveley	2-0

Third Round Second Replay

Hendon vs Leatherhead	0-2
(at Wycombe)	

Fourth Round

Ashington vs Woking	2-0
Bishop's Stortford vs Blyth Spartans	3-1
Ilford vs Dulwich Hamlet	1-1
Sutton United vs Leatherhead	0-1

Fourth Round Replay

Dulwich Hamlet vs Ilford	0-1

Semi-Finals

Ashington vs Bishop's Stortford	0-0
(at Sunderland)	
Ilford vs Leatherhead	1-0
(at Millwall)	

Semi-Final Replay

Bishop's Stortford vs Ashington	3-0
(at Brentford)	

Final

Bishop's Stortford vs Ilford	4-1
(at Wembley Stadium 20 April 1974)	

Attendance: 30,500

Bishop's Stortford: Moore, Gibson, Coombes, Lawrence, Still, Payne, Leakey, Dear, Bass, Smith, Murphy
Sub: Scott
Scorers: Lawrence, Murphy, Leakey, Smith (penalty)
Ilford: James, Bowhill, Bennett, Betson, Anderson, Day, Bookman, Butterfield, Drabwell, McDermid, Turley
Sub: Guiver
Scorer: Drabwell
Referee: D. Turner (Cannock)